App Quality
Secrets for Agile App Teams

Beta

Jason Arbon

Thanks to the patience of my wife Heather, and children Luca, Mateo, Dante, and Odessa who still think I work at Starbucks.

--Technarus

Who Should Read This Book

Everyone who cares about apps should read this book.

- **Developers** The nerds who spend their time focusing on Java namespaces and Objective-C protocols. The approach in this book is designed for improving quality in an agile and lean team environment.
- **Testers** Both the manual and automation test developers who live and breathe app quality. This book outlines the methods for discovering your app's weaknesses, how to quantify your app's quality, and effectively share these issues with the rest of the team.
- **Product Managers, Designers, Owners, VPs, CIOs, CMOs, CEOs** The folks defining the next generation of Apps, care about the bottom line, or how the app impacts their brand. The approach detailed in this book is specifically geared toward teams practicing agile or lead methodologies.
- **App Users** Yeah, those 2+Billion folks who use the apps we build. Customers who want a deeper understanding of what makes their apps tick and why apps sometimes fail at the exact wrong moment.

This book is not a deep-dive technical guide on how to install crash SDKs, sign your apps, or teach the fundamentals of user interface design. This book is designed to give everyone an overview of the major quality issues impacting modern app design, testing, and implementation, with tips and pointers to more resources. Given this wide audience, the book occasionally refers to things that are either too nerdy for some, or leaving others wanting for more detail. When it gets too nerdy or technical, just skip along, it is not important for later understanding. When it feels like the text is just getting to the technical details and then stops--follow the references and do a bit of searching around the web—Google.com and StackOverflow.com are your friends. Or, you can always ping me with a random question. The book aims to be of lasting value. The companies and apps referred to in the text are just examples and starting points for further exploration. The app world is changing fast. This book isn't a list of all services or apps, but shares a representative few of them. The hope was to write one book to build a common understanding of app quality across disciplines, and be the kernel of conversations between developers, testers, product owners, managers, and even users, about making better apps.

Content Outline

The book progresses through steadily increasing level of details and depth. Feel free to stop when you feel data overload, or skip ahead if you nod off because you've heard it already.

1. **Mobile App Quality Monsters**: Mobile apps have different quality issues than their Desktop and Web cousins. Explore the top ten mobile quality monsters that directly impact app quality.
2. **App Store Reviews and Quality Attributes**: An overview of the major types of user feedback common to all apps. Learn the best practices, including specific test cases, coding tips, design tips to address each major app quality attribute.
3. **App Store Analytics**: A deep dive on the data and patterns behind app store ratings. Some myths are debunked, and category-specific advice is shared.
4. **Mobile Test Automation**: The status of mobile test automation and current recommendations for when to automate, how much to automate, and which tools to use and which to avoid.
5. **Putting This All Together**: A deep dive on how to leverage app review analytics to build the quality strategy for agile teams. See this all in action, on a real world app.
6. **Future of App Quality**: A glimpse into the future of app quality to stay ahead of the curve.

A Note on Book Layout and Formatting: This book has been written with multi-platform and fragmentation in mind. The layout is extremely simple and designed to look sharp on the largest and the smallest of devices. There are no fancy tables, just text with simple images, just like very app should be designed. I've also avoided many of the authority-inducing footnotes, figure captions, page numbers, to keep things simple. Simple scales better—both up and down. When you open this book on your desktop, the text and images should flow nicely to the far corners of your monitor if you choose. If you are reading this on a printed page, please plant a tree, but realize this book still used a bit less ink to get the point across. Design all things for a fragmented world.

A Further Note on Detail: This book is designed to be an overview of the entirety of app quality. Many paragraphs in this book could warrant entire chapters, or even books to describe the tools, data, and best practices. If folks have questions or want pointers to more detail, feel free to email me at jarbon@gmail.com. Specific tools and test cases, developer tips and example apps are shown, but this is a very large space. Forgive any brevity, it is partly because my favorite Starbucks store closes at 9pm.

Book Readiness: As the world of apps is in constant flux and evolving quickly, I've made efforts to get this book out as fast as possible. There are some grammatical issues here and there—I hope they don't get in the way of folks learning how to make better apps. There are also many places I intend to place additional interviews with industry folks, but their thoughts are currently caught up in some marketing, legal and PR approval loops. The eBook will be updated, just like modern apps, as new grammatical bugs and features come in. This is a living eBook in the near term. If you purchased a printed copy, just contact me and I'm happy to get you the updates as they come in. An agile app book should also be agile. Consider this book a solid beta, but still a work in progress.

Forward

by Dr. James A. Whittaker (@docjamesw)

Modern software developers bear little resemblance to our forebears. We've forsaken their jackets and ties in favor of hoodies and t-shirts. We've quit their offices and cubicles to occupy hacker hostels and corner cafés. They had floppies and sneakernet. We have GitHub. They printed and stored; we share and post. They worked for big companies with good distribution channels. The world is our distribution channel. Where, with all these changes, do we stand with software testing?

Let's face it, the 1990s were the golden age of software testing. As an industry we were still figuring things out. Global or local data? File and variable naming conventions? Time constraints versus memory utilization. Library, procedure or inline code? Use or reuse? And the granddaddy of them all: how do we fix bugs that occur in the field when the only way to get bug reports is by phone or email and the only way to update the software is by mailing a new set of floppies? We were at once not very experienced in writing code and after shipping that code, fixing it was a really, really painful proposition.
No wonder we put so much time and effort into testing. We had no choice but to double check developers' work and try to ensure that as few bugs as possible made it into the released product.

Like I said, it was a golden age for software testers. Small chance of getting it right, large chance of expensive rework. Testers were the insurance policy no company could afford to decline.

But then the world changed. First it was the web that made software updates a small matter of refreshing a web page. Complicated updates were F5-ed into oblivion. And then along came mobile apps, which could collect their own user telemetry, create their own failure reports and prompt a user to update them when necessary. At the same time the risk of shipped defects was decreasing dramatically, so-called waterfall software development models were replaced with agile methods that created better code out-of-the-box and a collective intelligence around how to code and the body of knowledge of coding practices matured. The art of coding has become downright pedestrian.

Quality is no less important today, but achieving it requires a different focus than in the past. Testing is much less an actual role now as it is an activity that has blended into the other activities developers perform every day. Testing can now involve users at a level that it never could in the past. Who, after all, is the better judge of a bug: the user who is honestly trying to use the software to get work (or pleasure) done or a tester who has a preconceived (and unavoidably biased) notion of how the software is supposed to work? Why must a tester serve as the intermediary between the developer and the user when the user is only a click away?

Quality, and therefore testing, is not something separate from software development unless your software is going into a nuclear power plant or an airplane where it is difficult to recall. For the vast majority of app development on this planet, software testing is an activity within the development process and keeps happening after the software is deployed. Modern testing *is an activity* and doesn't require a separate role to perform it. It is time to bring quality into the 21st century and Jason Arbon is the first author I've seen who does this. In this book you will learn that testing is an activity (not a role) that can be seamlessly integrated into an agile development process using all the same tools you use today. You'll learn how to engage with early adopters to get their feedback and how to use that feedback to improve your product. You'll learn how to assess how your product is pleasing, or displeasing, your users. You'll learn how to make software testing such an integral part of software development that you'll often forget you are doing because it has become so familiar.

This is not your father's application development process. It is time to bring testing into the 21st century.

About the Author

Jason Arbon has worked in development, test and product manager roles at a wide range of companies. He's currently Director of Product and Engineering at Applause.com (formerly uTest.com), focusing on mobile apps and analytics to quantify quality. Applause.com handles the crowd-sourced testing of hundreds of well-known applications from Google, to Twitter, Microsoft, Netflix, Fox and HBO, and many high profile mobile startups.

Previously, Jason held test leadership and innovation roles at Google on projects such as personalized search on Google+, Chrome Browser, Chrome OS, Google Desktop, and Google Talk and lead the centralized test engineering team. Jason also worked on teams at Microsoft including Bing Search Relevance, Live QnA, WinFS, BizTalk Server, MSN, Windows CE and Exchange Server. Along the way, He co-founded a small social search start up, and worked at several small and mid-size companies. He also co-authored the book 'How Google Tests Software'. Jason's weekends are spent working on his quest to build the world's smartest mobile browser. He's received degrees in Electrical Engineering and Computer Engineering from the University of Utah.

Preface

Writing this book was a journey that began on an iPhone. This same book was later edited on an iPad, an Android phone, and even a desktop web version of the Quip app. I, for one, gladly welcome our new world of mobile apps.

My cab driver just missed ten pedestrians by inches and woke me out of a stupor. I'm writing this using a new mobile app called Quip, on my iPhone5s, in the middle of Shanghai. I had the thought to write a book on the topic of app quality, and suddenly realized I didn't have to wait until I got back to my laptop to start. I could use my iPhone, right there in the cab. Maybe I wouldn't have been so inspired by the time I got back to my laptop.

I'm writing now at Din Tai Fung, a restaurant at the base of the World Financial Center, the tallest building in China until the one next-door is finished. Today, you can work on a book, and practically anything else, while eating Dim Sum!

On the flight back from Shanghai, I had plenty of time to work on my iPad, typing away at the index and general message of this book. No laptop required, and the iPad didn't run out of battery.

I'm now writing this in a bar at a bar in San Francisco. I'm presenting at AnDevCon, a gathering of some of the geekiest Android developers on the planet tomorrow. And, you guessed it; I'll be walking to the podium with only my iPhone in hand to present. No laptop required.

Scarcity brings clarity. Modern apps are almost completely awesome, simple, and they are everywhere. They are often much easier to use than their distant desktop and web page cousins. These mobile devices with their small and slow keyboards, tiny screens and intermittent network connections have forced developers to make far more elegant, simple, fast, and robust applications. Users won't tolerate the time it takes for an app to load, let alone read how to use it. Users want their apps to do a few things very well, very quickly, and will rarely discover advanced or fancy features. These mobile apps are quick to find and easier to uninstall. They are inexpensive or even free. They have lots of promise. There are millions of them—but how good are they?

Star ratings and reviews tell us how good (or bad) these apps are. The best thing about this new app world is that there are tons of app reviews sitting in the app stores just waiting to be read and analyzed. App owners, whether they like it or not, have finally made contact with the voice of the user, and these users aren't all that happy with their apps.

This book aims to help app developers, testers, product owners, marketers and CEOs ensure their mobile apps are the best they can be. Frankly, mobile might soon be the only way many people in the world access your services, so it is a good idea to get started and get it right.

Where did this book come from?

I'm currently the Director of Product and Engineering at Applause.com (formerly uTest.com)—a company that tests mobile apps "in the wild". My team has been focused on mobile app quality, testing and analytics for several years. I've personally had the opportunity to learn from many thousands of test cycles performed on many hundreds of well-known apps. Our team consists of a few other ex-Googlers and ex-Bingers, so of course we have to crawl, index, search and analyze all the data in the app stores. Analyzing hundreds of millions of reviews for over a million applications, has given us additional insights into quality. We are sharing much of that data over on the website http://analytics.applause.com. I'm also an app developer. I live app quality. In my role at Applause, I've also spent quite a bit of time talking and working with top app development teams at both large and small companies and used those conversations to understand the state of app quality, development and design.

Like the last book I co-authored, "How Google Tests Software", there is nothing like the scale of sharing ideas in book form or the fun of running into people you have never met that are applying the lessons you so painfully learned.

This book is shorter, more direct, and more actionable just like a mobile app should be. This book exists to share what I've learned thus far and will be updated as I learn more. My world, and my kids' worlds, is filled with more and more apps every day--I want those apps to be great.

Introduction

Quality is an interesting word. Quality, like beauty, is the in the eye of the beholder. Quality used to mean that it worked as expected. With desktop software, users would get frustrated, restart the app, or load a backed up version of the file, and had nowhere to complain. With free web apps, users were a bit more tolerant with bugs as long as they were fixed quickly-they would refresh the page, or try a different browser. Software quality used to be measured by experts at test labs such as PC World, with many rows and columns comparing apps feature by feature. With mobile apps, quality has not only morphed to include many non-traditional things such as how pretty the user experience (UX) is, but simplicity and lack of features are the new 'it' and new user expectation. Quality has also grown in importance, visibility, and for better or worse, is now summarized as a single star rating with a few pieces of feedback from random folks you don't know.

Your app's quality, and perception of your app's quality, has never been more tenuous. In the days of desktop apps, there were a few major platforms to consider (OS and RAM), and with the web, a few flavors of browsers to worry about, and you usually had months of lead-time before your app reached your customers so you could test it out. Your mobile apps today live on devices you've never heard of, at screen resolutions that were insane a year ago, and LTE networks in countries you've never visited. Even the operating systems and new devices are released with zero notice. We'll cover how to keep up with all this change, and especially focus on how to stay current with minimal expense and time.

This book is relevant to all apps, mobile apps, native apps, desktop apps, web apps, apps for cars, and TVs, and watches, and even apps on platforms yet to be invented. What makes an app an app is that fact that it is distributed via a curated store, and users are able to post reviews of their experience with the app. At this time, most apps are mobile, and often mobile native apps, so many of the details, and data analytics below are taken from the Google Play and Apple App Stores—but, most all of it is applicable to all apps.

The software quality game has changed dramatically with the rise of app stores, but most don't realize it yet. Lets explore what has changed, how to deal with it, and where we expect all this to lead us in the future.

Apologies First

Wow! I resisted typing "App-ologies". I'd like to get these issues out of the way before we begin.

Highlighted Apps

Throughout this book, we will explore the quality, or lack thereof, in several top apps. The goal is to use these apps as examples that many readers can relate to, as many have these very apps installed on their devices today. These apps are also used to demonstrate that even well funded and top app teams struggle with app quality. Knowing that top app teams also struggle should make the indie app developers feel a little bit better about their own app quality. Forgive me if your app is featured for bad. Love me if your app is featured for good.

Applause.com and uTest.com Promotion

Applause.com and uTest.com references are littered throughout this book. Applause is prominent in that its very existence stemmed from my desire to understand the app stores via review analytics. Applause was designed as a platform for understanding the data behind app quality, and most of that data just isn't available anywhere else. uTest.com is of course the worlds largest app test team, and I have unfettered access to the bugs and tests and learning from that community of testers. I don't know how else I could have efficiently gathered best practices from large numbers of testers more efficiently. Where I can, I point to other sources of information and have gone out of my way to bring in industry feedback, thoughts, and stories. Simply put, this book is not intended as marketing fodder.

Section I: Mobile App Quality Monsters

Some folks look at mobile app quality and say, "It is just another platform", or "It is just like….". They are wrong. A different vector of quality issues impact mobile apps. The app world is different than the days Web and Desktop applications. Some things remain the same, but many are new, or more far more important in the mobile world. Your app's quality is highly dependent on these 10 app-specific quality monsters. Ignore them at your peril.

These monsters are chasing after your app's quality:

1. App Deployment and Distribution
2. Device Fragmentation and State
3. Users
4. Real World
5. Metrics
6. Competition
7. Security and Privacy
8. User Interface
9. Agile Teams
10. Reviews

Below, we walk through each major quality monster and outline how the different team members/roles can work to defend your app's quality.

Quality Monster: App Deployment and Distribution

"Now along comes the potential creative destruction brought by a different distribution methodology, the Internet." --Barry Diller

With desktop applications and web sites, apps shipped when the team decided to ship. Some teams shipped once a year, others shipped hourly. When a team deploys through an app store, teams have far less control. If users find nasty bugs after launch, the fixes go out when the app store feels the time is right--which can be days later. App teams have less control over the presentation of the app. The app stores allow for a few screenshots, the app's icon, and one big text box in which to cram all your marketing and user messaging. The app store also happily hosts all the negative feedback and puts a star rating next to your company's brand for hundreds of millions of people to discover. The good thing is that you don't have to worry much about the mechanics of deployment anymore, but that luxury comes with a price.

Tips for App Testers

Yellow Pages Check the app listing details before and after your app is published. Check the content, images, and update text, as this is the first thing potential users see—Any quality issues here will reflect on the quality of the app. Check to be sure that the text isn't just accurate, but sounds modern and engaging. Screenshots used to be just that, screenshots. Today, app store screenshots are marketing materials that are overlaid with text to explain further hype and explain the app. Don't deploy an awesome app only to have it displayed on a mediocre download page in the app store.

N'Sync The app stores don't always update your app's content at the same time as your app is available for download. Check the new version number to make sure the build you think should have been deployed is the one that gets downloaded. Keep marketing folks from declaring victory and posting stories about the updated app's UI, if the app store entry still looks like the old one.

Final check If your app requires a sign in, or takes a lot of time to add content in order to test out major app functionality, you will need to share that account information with the app store so their approval team can test out your app quickly. It is in your interest to make sure their testing is as easy as possible since any questions from the approval team can add a day or more of delay.

Upgrades not Downgrades Test your app in upgrade scenarios. Remember that some users may even be upgrading from very old versions. Upgrades are known for losing users data. The Starbucks app is suffering from this as I type. Their app removed some seemingly useless part of the app where you could create your favorite drinks. Their new app version simply removes (or doesn't display) this old data. Even though the old version of the app had many users complaining that they can't do anything interesting like ordering with these drink profiles, users will still cry foul when it goes missing after an update. If you do deprecate or retire old functionality, be sure your users won't be too upset and message this transition within the app.

Starbucks
 Food & Drink | Applause Score: 36/100

Review, 1-Star, Starbucks iOS "Starbucks - you blew it. My custom drinks are gone! Where did you put the food and drink info? I liked knowing what went into the drinks, customizing and knowing calories. Bring them back, please!" -MaElwood

Review, 1-Star, Starbucks iOS "Where'd my custom drinks go??? I miss being able to have my custom drinks! I used this feature ALL the time after having something really good I like. Not liking the update. Two stars because its only saving grace is a cleaner UI" -Stefi

Be One with the User: Shortly after launch, and even weeks after launch, download and install a fresh version of your app directly from the app store onto your own device. Yes, you think you tested it before launch, but what matters is the app version that users download. Make sure that there aren't any server, protocol, or backend changes that might have impacted your app's first-launch experience. Continually check that the app download experience works for real-world users.

It's a Small World App Store distribution means your app can be deployed around the world with a single click. App teams are often in a race to reach the entire world. Test for basic globalization and localization issues as early as possible.

Globalization Question every piece of text in your app. Would a longer German translation of the word fit in that dialog or button? Ask your developers for a pseudo-localized build that contains strings representing the worst-case string translation and rendering scenarios for string length and special characters, and see where your app's UX fails. Here is a <u>link to a great Google blog post on pseudo-loc builds</u>: (<u>http://google-opensource.blogspot.com/2011/06/pseudolocalization-to-catch-i18n-errors.html?spref=bl</u>)

Localization Make sure your app is translated correctly and is compatible with locale-specific issues such as date, time, weights and measures. Switch your OS's locale—test that your app does the right thing with different date formats, keyboards, characters, etc.

Tips for App Developers

Signing Paperwork The app stores require you to sign your builds so they know it is from your team. This protects everyone from cloned or dangerous apps rampaging through the app stores. But app signing, particularly for iOS, can be very confusing, painful. Lean on other folks in the community when you get stuck on some part of the signing process. Stack Overflow.com is your friend— sometimes more than the app store's developer documentation. Everyone suffers. There should be some solace in that.

Tips for App Product Managers

O Canada Don't launch in the US (or your major target market) first. Deploy your app to a market that is linguistically and culturally similar as your primary market. This lets you get feedback, and test out your app, and marketing materials, in a hidden corner of the app store. Once you know things are going well in Canada, cross the border.

Curmudgeons App teams are always infatuated with their new app versions, but users don't always agree. There are always people that just don't like change. This is more of a problem if you don't regularly update your app as users may not be expecting an update. The app stores have moved to automatic updates, so updates are even more jarring as users randomly wake up to a new app the next time it launches. Be sure to think through the user's transition between the old and new app versions, perhaps even adding some text or intro screens to welcome users to the new app. Showing off new features and how to perform common tasks when they first launch the new version can go a long way to keeping users happy. Keep these introductions short though, as they can also get in the way. Don't shock your users with a dramatically different app--boil them slowly.

Sword of Damocles You are never sure your app will be accepted into the app store. Some apps are rejected, or even pulled from the app stores. You can read all the app store rules, regulations and UX guidelines, test the app thoroughly, but you can never be sure you will pass the approval process. The app stores deliberately keep this process opaque. Everything you add to your app increases the chance of a quality issue or feature that will get your app stuck in the approval process. Every time your app is updated, you run the risk of being inspected by a different app store approval officer, with fresh eyes looking for trouble. Even when the app is blocked from the app store, you often can't talk about it because of your NDA.

The app store review processes does find quality, usability, and integration issues. This can be a little embarrassing, but they are quick to fix. If there are features that you worry about getting approved, just ship early versions of your app to discover rejection as early as possible. You should also avoid doing things that similar apps have been banned for in the past: using reserved buttons for your app's function (e.g. using the iPhone's volume button for taking pictures), or selling placement in the app store's top app lists. It is also just smart to make sure your app is of high quality and intuitive for app store review folks to breeze through the approval process. Don't be the squeaky wheel.

Countdown Accidental launches happen. When you set a date and locale in the app store developer dashboard for your future release, be careful. There are many examples of an app accidentally launching early because the wrong date or locale was entered. Be careful. Check your app store dashboards like a hawk.

No Quick Returns App teams can't deploy fixes on a whim, at least not on iOS. Even on Android, your users aren't usually on Wi-Fi, so they can be stuck with a bad build for a while. Updates with bug fixes take time, so only ship quality apps in the first place. There are expedited app reviews available for iOS. You might be granted one if you have a strong case. Some cases that justify expedited reviews: being a popular app, or showing that a bad bug will impact many users, or if you are a fledgling startup and you are launching at a conference the next morning. You can only use this get out of jail free card so many times so use it wisely. Even when you can get an expedited update, it is often still 24 or 36 hours for that new build to make its way to your users. If you do try to revert to the previously approved version of your app in a panic, test the version downgrade scenario first. Bad things happen when walking backwards. Only push high quality builds in the first place.

Hide in Plain Sight Don't put your app in the app store if it is not intended for the general public. Confused and poor reviews will start appearing from random people. If you are building an app for your internal sales force, or internal business app, get an enterprise-signing key. Just ask for it. Apply for an iTunes enterprise account here (https://developer.apple.com/support/ios/enterprise.html). Google play calls it the private channel (https://support.google.com/a/answer/2494992). Now you can deploy your app internally without fear of confused public app store reviews.

Staging When you deploy new versions of your app, it is best to stage your roll out. That means upgrading 1% of your users. Then let it sit for a day or two and see if anything bad happens. Then 5%, then 10%, until you get 100% and you have fully updated everyone. If you see any issues, fix them, and then update the folks that saw the issue before rolling out to more users. This helps avoid catastrophic issues from impacting all your users at once, and avoids many of the same negative reviews. Google Play supports staged rollouts. iOS doesn't support staged rollouts yet, but you can leverage complicated A/B testing methods, to achieve much the same effect. For iOS staging, you need to parameterize your app's code, and conditionally enable or disable different features and code paths—not easy, but it is possible. Facebook built and shared the A/B testing framework called Airlock (https://code.facebook.com/posts/520580318041111/airlock-facebook-s-mobile-a-b-testing-framework/). Stage your deploys to avoid the widespread plague of bugs or bad features from infecting all your users at once.

Quality Monster: Device Fragmentation and State

"If you thought the advent of the Internet, the spread of cheap and efficient information technology, and the growing fragmentation of the consumer market were all going to help smaller companies thrive at the expense of the slow-moving giants of the Fortune 500, apparently you were wrong." --James Surowiecki

Most apps live on tablets or phones. Yes, some live on desktops and some even live in web browsers like Chrome or Firefox. But all the action is on tablets and phones. Mobile devices come in more physical varieties than PC's today: CPU, RAM, screen DPI, resolution, buttons, ports, and physical buttons. Often your apps are running on devices you've never heard of, in countries where you didn't think your app was available. These devices are running a wide variety of Operating System (OS) versions with OEM customizations. The OS powering these devices is also mean to apps. Web and Desktop applications did what the developer asked of them. If an app spun in a tight loop like a while(1) { cout << "yippee"; }, the desktop, laptop or browser would happily slow your system down to a crawl. Not on mobile. The mobile OSs look for an excuse to kill your app. These devices are as powerful as many Desktop PCs, but if your app uses too much RAM or doesn't respond to touches immediately, your app will be closed by the OS and your users will blame your app. Test on a variety of devices, OS versions, and keep your app's memory footprint to a minimum, and never slow the user, or the system, down.

Mobile apps also keep state information on the device—much more than web apps. The game-save data, lists of in-app purchases, music files, sign-in information, draft documents, and much more often lives on the device. Some of this this data stays even after the app is uninstalled. Some of this data might have been left behind from a two-year-old version of an app. Never assume a clean device state, it is a large source of quality issues. Today's mobile apps live in a fragmented and dangerous world of devices with lots of state.

Tips for App Testers

Fast Forward When your app updates itself, it better not surprise the user with a radically new UI, lose functionality, or clear their data. Make the upgrades are smooth. When you think you have an awesome new UI, make sure the app walks the users through the transition. The user just opened your new app version to get something done; you just slowed them down, so you need to quickly ramp users on the new app changes. If you are removing any functionality, even seldom-used functionality, someone out there uses it, likes it and will complain when it is gone. Be careful about removing things, and when you do, tell them why. When you are beta testing, and dogfooding, install the old app, play with the app to set a bunch of state, then upgrade to the newer build. Make sure the user's sign in information isn't lost, their pictures are still there, the default settings made it through the upgrade, and the spot where they were last listening to that audio book is remembered. It is tempting to only focus on the future but you need to bring your users along with you.

Flippy: Start the app in all possible device states. Use the app in every device state. Change these device states while in the middle of using the app. Often apps assume if something was working a minute, or even milliseconds ago, it is still working. Apps will often get confused and crash, or perform strangely when the device or system state changes underneath them. Users get devices into these states accidentally, deliberately, and by just going about their day—apps need to deal with all sorts of device state. Here is a list of device states you should consider flipping during testing:

Networking
Location services/GPS
Power
Battery level
Background applications
Notifications Permissions and Settings
Privacy settings
Game Center and Google Play Games services access
Screen brightness
Social network authentication and authorization
Bluetooth
Sounds
Volume
Headphones plugged in/out
Full/empty storage
Incoming calls
Every physical button on devices

Note For exhaustive, but efficient testing, consider using the pair-wise testing approach http://en.wikipedia.org/wiki/All-pairs_testing

Busy Signal Make the device busy. Run many other apps in the background, especially similar and competitive apps, as they will consume similar resources. Make the app fight for the resources it

needs. See how it deals with timeouts due to networking, or CPU load. See how it competes with other apps downloading content and saving it to the same flash bank at the same time. Users often put their phones into extreme conditions--make sure your app holds up.

The Dirty When performing manual, and especially automated testing, keep a few machines around that you call "The Dirty". Don't ever wipe the state of these devices; upgrade the apps, upgrade the OS, but never clean it. Most real world devices are very dirty with old app state, OS upgrades, and are rarely rebooted or reset. Test your app on a device that is dirtier than your users' devices.

Undermine: It happens. Occasionally the cell carriers let users update their OS version a year or so after Google or Microsoft releases an update. Test your app as the OS is upgraded underneath your app. You may discover that your app's manifest said it can only run on version 5, but the OS just upgraded to version 6. The app might be flagged as incompatible—not a great experience for your users. Apps can also suffer from incompatibility with new API implementations, new OS requirements, or finding that an API the app depends on was removed. This is a relatively rare occurrence, but it is a monster as it can mean large swaths of your user base seeing this issue at the same time and your app being disabled. Test your app via several OS upgrade paths and make sure it is as forward compatible with future OS releases as possible. Keep an ear to the ground and watch industry blogs that talk about any major changes or release notes with the OS's while they are in beta—and try your app on those beta OS builds.

Voltron Devices with swappable hardware components are coming soon. Check that your app can survive the swapping of components it depends on. The world of app quality is about to get more complicated when these phones hit the market. Google's Project Ara phone is just one example. While your app is in the middle of taking a photo, remove the camera component. Or, add a second camera. See how the app behaves when anything can be added or removed dynamically.

Live It The team building the app should be using the app continuously. Distribute the latest builds to everyone on the team (aka Dogfooding), and with the larger company. Check if they use it. Really. If folks aren't helping with quality, they should be. If they aren't interested in your app—why do they work there? Many large companies have VPs that send out 'install it, or be shamed' emails and they tend to be effective in getting employees to install apps. This will deliver a good level of coverage in device state and fragmentation depending on your companies size. There are many tools such as Testflightapp.com, hockyapp.net, and sdk.applause.com that make it easy to distribute these builds, collect crashes, feedback and device information. Your team and company should be using your pre-production builds.

Share It Give your early adopters a peek and a voice. Share the next version of your app with your early adopter crowd. Not everyone is an early adopter, but most apps have a small set of folks that would gladly trade in a little bit of quality for a peek at the next version, and perhaps a chance to influence your teams' feature and bug decisions. Google Play Store supports has a basic beta program and the usual suspects can also be used to support Beta programs: Testflightapp.com, hockyapp.net, and sdk.applause.com. Too often companies think the next version of their app is so earth shattering that they must keep it under wraps—that's rarely the case and adds to overall quality risk. The best part of the Google Play alpha and beta support is that it keeps the feedback from early users out of the public app store listings, so you can safely get feedback without affecting your star rating. Share with your users and they'll help you build a better app.

Three's a crowd Large testing communities can be great for discovering issues because they have large variance in device fragmentation and state. These devices come with real world user state. Crowd testing services, such as http://www.utest.com, can have over a 100,000 people in their testing community, with all sorts of devices in all sorts of states, in all sorts of places, with all sorts of people. Since this is a testing community, the bug reports are professional with detailed bug reports including device hardware and state information, along with detailed reproduction steps (versus users vaguely complaining in the app store).

Heat up the Cloud Run your formal regression test passes and bug reproductions on devices in the cloud. Many progressive app teams started building out labs for their manual and automated testing, but these quickly became cumbersome and expensive as the number of new devices accelerated in the past couple of years. Don't repeat that mistake. Go directly to the cloud. PerfectoMobile.com gives you access to a wide range of devices and you can interact with the device via your web browser. Perfecto means you don't need to buy all these devices yourself. These devices are particularly good at enabling reproduction and debugging of issues across the fragmented device world. AppThwack.com and Appurify.com give API access to run your test automation on hundreds of different devices. AppThwack also has a service they call 'frictionless testing' where you give them your app and they automatically installs it on hundreds of devices, launches the app, and then sends thousands of taps, swipes, and gestures into your app and lets you know if it finds any crashes. It is a fast and easy way to see how your app performs under pressure. For manual or automated testing, use the cloud.

Pretend Most development environments come with device simulators or emulators that create virtual copies of a wide range of device configurations and state—right on your laptop. The Android emulator lets you toggle about anything you like: screen dimensions, DPI, networking, GPS/location, etc. Most major device aspects a can be set for quick testing. Nothing substitutes for the real thing, but the speed and convenience of virtual devices can speed up both testing and reproduction of issues. Android's emulator is notoriously slow, but luckily a few startups have answered with super fast emulators of their own. If you find yourself taking a nap while the Android Emulator is waking up, try Genymode's emulator—it is lightning fast and most developers swear by it. The convenience of an emulator is awesome for basic app testing, but don't let it substitute for real machines in your testing.

Listen Listen to what your users are saying. The text of many app reviews and social networking posts contain clues about device-specific issues. Read the reviews and look for issues. Your users are trying to help you isolate and reproduce issues, just listen to them.

Evernote
Productivity | Applause Score: 87

Review, 1-Star, Evernote Android: "919 error on install. Samsung galaxy S4 mini" –Joao Ramos

Review, 1-Star, Evernote Android: "Horrible. Samsung galaxy s1 Keeps crashing and asking to restart the phone"– Eunsoo Yang

And, some users even provide crazily complex repro scenarios.

Review, 1-Star, Evernote Android: "FIVE DAYS AND STILL WAITING FOR A FIX!!!!!. Devices / OS: Samsung GalTab 10.1 P7500 / 3.2 & Google Samsung Galaxy Nexus / 4.2.2 - Problem: after update last week home screen widget stopped updating changes made on pc (which confirmed sync). Drilling down discovered that problem was that sync in app itself is broken. -- Attempted Solutions (from EN Support): 1) logoff / reboot (they snuck in 5.1 to 5.1.1 update here) / resign in / let sync, did initial sync then just sat there for hrs doing no comms w/ cloud 2) de-install / reboot / re-install / reboot / resign in / let sync then just sat there for hrs doing no comms w/ cloud 3) have let devices run for 3 days now and no sync on either -- Conclusion: 1 device / OS is an anomaly, 2 devices / OS versions is a pattern (especially happening to same person), friends having same issues is A MAJOR PROBLEM -- Current Status: last communication from support was "We are looking into it" w/ no acknowledgement of problem -- THIS NEEDS TO BE ADMITTED TO BY EVERNOTE AND FIXED!!!!!!" --Stefan Jon Silverman

Tips for App Developers

Wake Up Carefully Load your data carefully. When your code wakes up and restores state from the local store, or a server, be very cautious. Try, catch, and validate everything. Remember if there are older app state formats you've used on previous versions. Users may not always upgrade from version 3 to version 4, sometimes it is version 1 to version 4. Too often apps get into a bad state where they crash on launch and the user simply can't enter the app to correct the issue, and their only option is to delete your app. If you are lucky they try downloading again, but often they are just gone. Validate all data, and handle every exception as gracefully as possible.

Stay off the Radar Use as little memory as possible to stay tiny and avoid being shutdown. Assume the device has very little memory. Aggressively free memory when you don't need it, and allocate as little as possible by paging large resources only on-demand, and incrementally. Test your app in low memory simulators. Use the memory profilers and analyzers that come with your platform IDEs. When profiling, use your app aggressively, and leave the app running for long time to catch slow and sneaky leaks. Stay off the radar and you might avoid being shutdown.

Import Ant Never trust any call to a 3rd party API or system service. Too often developers check for things like permissions, network, etc. and then assume they are still there for later calls. Always assume these calls will fail—because they will at some point.
System, Network, and 3rd Party APIs are especially flaky on mobile so wrap every call in exception handling and smart-recovery/retry logic. State can even change between lines of your code, so wrap all external calls in larger rollback and user friendly wrappers. There are many solid 3rd party networking and other libraries with much of this built in. There are simply too many to list here, but if you aren't using them, your app is living dangerously. A good rule of thumb is if you are making a direct call to an API you don't own you are in trouble.

Manifest Destiny Use your app's manifest XML files and plists to prevent install on devices that don't meet your app's requirements, or devices that you haven't tested yet, or configurations you haven't thought of yet. Make sure your manifest supports future OS versions if that's the right thing for you, or your app could get stuck in no-mans-land during a future OS upgrade.

Tips for App Product Managers

Flow Around it Give error flow as much consideration as the functional paths. Design for version upgrade flows. Design for UX and flow where the network is missing, battery is low, device is out of storage, or data pasted from another app that your app has no idea how to process. Make sure the user knows what going on—failing silently is a quick way to really frustrate the user. If you let the user know what call failed, or what went wrong, they might be able to remedy it by turning off airplane mode, or re-enabling social network sign ins or granting your app location or notification permissions again. Assume failures and design the flow to let the user know, and help them resolve it. A little bit of fun messaging can go a long way too—let your app team's personality show through.

Rally the Troops Organize dogfood and beta programs. Use carrots and sticks to get folks to use the builds and track their app usage. sdk.applause.com has been used to power corporate Betas with over 100,000 invites, track usage, crashes, and even has a nifty in-app bug filing utility. With the Applause SDK installed, just shake the app and it will take a screenshot and capture all the device state info (battery level, network conditions, memory usage, OS, hardware, etc.). Other SDKs and services include TestFairy.com (Android only), and AppSee.com (iOS only) also help track what users did, and where they went in beta builds. The earlier you incorporate the feedback into your sprint planning, the less expensive the changes will be and the more time you have to evaluate the changes.

Quality Monster: Users

"Sometimes it is a little bit like being a politician. We have work to do in understanding our users' sentiments." --Meg Whitman

App users are picky. On the web, we forgive bugs by 'refreshing' the browser, and blame the slow network. Desktop applications were always clunky things where the user expected to read a manual before using. On mobile devices, users launch your app while in line at Starbucks and expect to understand how to play the game and be done by the time they get their coffee and put their phone back in their pocket. If they can't use your app with just their thumb while carrying their Grande Vanilla Macchiato while walking to the bus stop, they get frustrated and delete you. Your app has very little time to impress on first use, and very little time to get most actions done. Design and test for this. You also don't get to pick your user. You can't just distribute your app to existing paid customers for your niche product--anyone can download it, get confused, and complain about it. App users even complain about wanting to pay for apps that are free, but ad supported. You just can't win them all, but you should try. On mobile devices, it is far tougher to make users happy.

Tips for App Testers

Random Audience Assume no single demographic or magic persona will use your app. The app stores are too widely distributed. Everyone finds your app. Grandmas sometimes find tinder. Design for your target user, but be sure the app store entry describes the app and target audience well to dissuade folks that won't like your app. Mismatches between apps and users are like bad relationships and the breakup often happens in the form of a 1-star review.

Tough Love Get feedback from your friends, family and co-workers. If you don't have many friends you can rent them. Leverage services like UserTesting.com or Applause.com where you can pay to get people in the real world to give you feedback on your app. UserTesting.com gives you short videos from paid folks. Applause.com can get you full usability expert evaluations.

Tips for App Developers

Design for Change Design your code for change. Great web and desktop code is modular, but in mobile it is essential. You will get great feedback on your app—you want to be able to quickly pivot, take the feedback, change the UX or functionality and get back out there for even more iterative feedback. If you find yourself saying, "that's good feedback, but it would be too expensive or risky to make the change", it is time to refactor your code. At the end of the day, the user, and the rest of your team doesn't care how elegant your code is, but they do care how quickly you iterate.

Tips for App Product Managers

Be Social on Social Engage app users on social media. If they have feedback or comments on Twitter, or Facebook—reply and say 'great feedback', and follow up when you update your app. Create a two-way conversation with your users, or be at the mercy of their angry tweets about how you never listen. Do avoid any nutty exchanges with nutty folks—but that's what being a smart PR person is all about.

Cold Hard Facts Check your app's engagement data. Flurry.com and Google Analytics are great tools to understand what users are doing, or not doing, in your app. If you just added a great new feature—see if anyone has discovered it. If users are spending a lot of time in a feature that was an afterthought—invest in that area. Analytics can tell you were users went in your app, as well as the demographics of your users—it might note be quite what you expect. Be sure to keep your engagement data in mind when considering new features, UX, and where to engage them.

Just Ask Like dating, there are many of indirect ways to find out if someone is interested in you, but you can always just ask. Apptentive.com and UserVoice.com are great examples of user engagement SDKs and frameworks. Apptentive lets you do awesome things like 'if a user bails out of a flow, twice, ask them what is wrong'. Have a 'help' button where they can engage your team in a quick conversation. You can also roll out surveys to ask users what they like, don't like, and what dreamy features they wish your app supported. Whether you roll your own infrastructure, or leverage another service, use your app to engage your real users.

Review Analysis We'll get into this a lot more in the second half off this book, but reviews can help you get into the mind of your user (or users of your competitor's app). When reading app reviews, you will hear their wants, musings, wishes, rants, confusion, and even love for your app--much more on this later. You might as well keep reading if you made it this far.

Quality Monster: The Real World

Mike: It's too late! We're banished, genius! We're in the human world!
--Monsters, Inc.

Web and Desktop applications used to simply run in a web browser or desktop OS with a large power supply, steady network, connected to mice and keyboards, and sitting on a desk. Modern mobile apps run on devices that parents throw from the front to back seat to appease their whining daughter. Apps run on devices that are in planes, trains, and automobiles. They are also on construction sites, at the beach, on top of mountains, and on cruise ships. House cats claw at apps because they show pictures of fish. Apps are used on slow networks, switching cell towers at 70mph, or plugged into an alarm clock, or are the alarm clock. Apps run on devices that aren't plugged in and just about out of power. They run on devices full of other apps playing audiobooks in the background or trying to access the camera at the same time. You need to think about all the ways your app will be used in the real world.

Tips for App Testers

Get Out Get out of the office. Literally. Test your app at the mall, while you are being driven around town, at a park, while out for a run, in a restroom at the airport, and in head shop in Boulder,

Colorado, or at a poker table at the Bellagio in Vegas. Is your app easy to use? Ask other people at the coffee shop to take a look at it. How does it look in the bright sun at the beach? Expense some interesting trips in the name of app quality—you are welcome.

Law of Large Numbers Leverage crowd testing services and beta users. Do some test runs with Appluase.com, or UserTesting.com, and get feedback from folks using the devices in places outside of your lab, on real devices, with real users. The more the merrier. You will want your regression test case lists executed by many people with many different opinions and context, on many devices. If you only ask your friends what they think, your app will only appeal to other nerds. You will also want your exploratory testing done my many different people and devices—these testers will try different things and catch different issues than your team would have found. Be warned though, these folks will help you find functional issues, but you can still be surprised in production since these crowd testers aren't always the exact target audience of your app, nor have they paid for the app, nor will they live with your app like your end users will. You should find as many crowd and beta testers are you can, but it will never be enough.

Definition: Exploratory Testing. Exploratory testing is an approach to software testing that is concisely described as simultaneous learning, test design and test execution. Cem Kaner, who coined the term in 1983, now defines exploratory testing as "a style of software testing that emphasizes the personal freedom and responsibility of the individual tester to continually optimize the quality of his/her work by treating test-related learning, test design, test execution, and test result interpretation as mutually supportive activities that run in parallel throughout the project." --Wikipedia

Tips for App Developers

Code outside At least code at a cafe from time to time. It will make you think about where your app will really be used and the people who will be using it. Anything about your app that seems fragile is fragile, and the real world will expose it.

Tips for App Product Managers

You are here Your app should know where your app is at all times. Your app should also know what your user is doing. Make your app smarter based on this knowledge. Is the user moving fast? Maybe larger buttons or a simpler, 'driving' UX would help? Outside? Try a color scheme that works better outside? In the Dark? Transition the app's UI to white-on-black so you don't hurt your user's eyes. Think of all the ways your app's UX, flow, functionality could be optimized by leveraging all the data you have at your disposal in modern app development. Your app is not an island.

Quality Monster: Metrics

Wazowski. Always watching. Always.
--Monsters, Inc

The metrics monster is actually your friend--as long as you two are talking. There are so many easy-to-add and easy-to-view ways to track your apps. Collect and report on all crashes, check. Track your revenue and download counts, even versus other apps, check. See where your users are in the world in real-time, check. Collect feedback from users from within the app, check. See how many users keep your app after 30 days, check. View the performance of all your web requests, and your server reliability, check. If you aren't tracking all these things, and checking the data they generate, realize that your competitors are looking their own data closely. If you aren't talking with the metrics monster, he's helping your competitors get better, faster.

Tips for App Testers

Wag the Dog Ignore your test case pass/fail metrics—they are trailing metrics. OK, don't ignore them completely, but there is far more valuable data related to quality in all the engagement info, the device info, performance data, questions you ask of your users etc. If the usage of a feature suddenly drops—it is likely a functional or usability bug. If usage goes up, it could also be signs of trouble. The Google Chrome team once identified an issue with the JavaScript history.back() method because they noticed the usage of the back button had increased—people were clicking the button over and over again because it was toast. If you don't have time to build out a large suite of performance metrics, at least get your developer to add <u>New Relic</u> to your mobile and backend builds and immediately see what is slowing your app down. Consider if your app is too slow, or fast enough for release based on real data. Seek ways of getting quality data to your team before they have to do it themselves.

The Stick Use metrics to bolster your case. If you have an important bug that folks just don't seem to pay attention to, use data to back your case. Share a graph showing that performance is dropping over time. Share app store reviews complaining about how confusing the new profile page is for users. Show the product owner they need to prioritize quality by plotting a declining star rating over time. Metrics can be your friend if you use them to bolster your case. It is hard to argue with the facts.

The Carrot Quality isn't just about finding bugs, quality is about knowing what is going right with the app too. When you find that your app is crashing less often than it used to, let the team know— that's awesome news. Notice that performance is improving based on metrics? Congratulate the developers that made it happen, or the PM who provided the prioritization to get it done during the last sprint. Notice that app store complaints for an issue you escalated have disappeared—share the good news. Watch all your app's metrics and look for the positive. The carrot often works better than the stick.

Tips for App Developers

Instrument In mobile there are SDKs and tools to measure everything you can imagine about your app. Use them. Crashes, engagement, bug reporting, user communication. Most SDKs even enable custom event logging (a.k.a Breadcrumbs). Breadcrumbs let you see what internal app events led up to a crash, or other failures. If you don't measure it, you will have a tough time improving it. You are a computer nerd and computers are about data. Great developers love having more metrics to validate and guide their work. Most SDKs take less than an hour to add to your app. Adding these metric SDKs to your builds produce dashboards for your PM and testers, and empower them without bugging you with meetings or emails full of questions. Most top app teams have multiple SDKs tracking the details of how their apps are behaving and being used. Do the same.

Schrodinger's Quality Now that you are sold on adding a bunch of SDKs to your builds, here comes the warning label: "Add as few as you can bear". With each new SDK added to your build, you add complexity, and the complexity can interfere with the very app quality you are working to measure:

- **Updates** Congratulations, you just added a dependency—perhaps the most dangerous and annoying thing you can do in software development. Third party SDKs will have their own update cadence, and you will have to track these changes and update your code.
- **IT and Legal Buy-in** When you add software dependencies, it often adds to the legal complexity of your software licensing, and IT processes for approval. If adding an SDK doesn't add these burdens, that's probably a sign that you are running a bit too freely with your mobile app development culture.
- **Build and Runtime Issues** Sometimes, 3rd party SDKs and libraries contribute to build or runtime errors that aren't your fault, or expose issues with your own code. Most build issues will arise at the time of integration, but not all. Things like namespace overlap, or opaque protocol extensions can confuse debugging of issues long after the SDK was added. Some SDKs have even included binaries that app developers often include in their own apps. The Facebook SDK once included a common JSON parsing utility that caused confusing link-time issues, and forcing developers to use the SDK's version of the library. Be cautious. Use SDKs that are widely used, updated with fixes, and backed by great teams that are willing to help debug with you.
- **Performance** Most every SDK adds a performance issue to your app. These SDKs work by collecting and storing information on the device, then pushing that data back up to servers for analysis. This data can be large (or small) depending on how clever the SDK team is. These network calls can happen at the best of times, or the worst of times, for your app. Again, the SDK's impact on your app's quality depends on the expertise and focus of the SDK team behind it. If you check only one performance issue, check your app's startup performance with and with out the SDK included, and make you are OK with the metrics vs. performance tradeoff.
- **Big Binaries** Another reason to avoid SDKs is that they add to your app's size. The larger your app's size, the

longer the time between the user's intent to use your app, and the time they can engage with it as it takes time to download the app before the user can launch it. Users care about this, and can be source of significant abandonment. App stores and devices will also block the download of large apps (50-100MB) over non-Wi-Fi networks. Some users never connect to Wi-Fi, or, they will forget they wanted your app by the time they get to Wi-Fi, so your app's bulk can filter a large number of users. To address some of these issues, the more advanced SDK's have two versions; one for production and one for staging and testing. The staging and testing versions are often full of features and bulky, but the production ones are slim and include only the absolute basics required for their work. When in doubt, pick the smallest SDK footprint that delivers the value you need.

- **One size fits all** The market isn't mature enough to have a couple perfect solutions that do most of what you need. There has been some feature consolidation among SDKs recently, but it has resulted in poorer SDK quality. The engagement/click analytics SDKs are adding support for crash reporting. The crash collection folks are adding clicks and breadcrumbs. The performance folks are adding the other two services. As you'd expect, when development teams are adding features outside their core competency, they don't perform quite as well as an SDK produced by a team focused on that single service. At this point in time, the security, binary size, and network performance varies widely, and is changing monthly. Today, apps should stick to using single-purpose SDKs and whenever possible disable non-core functionality of the do-it-all SDKs. This might change in the coming years, but for now, stick with the professionals. Two very popular, SDKs add and additional 5 network calls and up to 10 seconds of latency to launch timing. Be careful out there.
- **Security and Privacy** Security is a real concern with 3rd party Services and SDKs. First, be careful what data you log to the service. That data may be written to less secure device log locations than you might realize. That data

might be pushed over non-SSL connections. That data might be pushed to another server that doesn't meet your SOC2 or HIPPA requirements. Also, hope that that third party service doesn't get hacked and expose your users data in detail, or even in aggregate. Be careful that you don't accidentally bundle a test version of an SDK that shows your users location down to the feet, when your app legally promises not to use location data more detailed than the city level. Know what the SDK does with your data, and use it cautiously.

- **Instrumentation** An emerging trend is SDK addition post-build. That is, instead of the pain of downloading binaries and adding lines of code to your app, the SDK binary can be added after your build is complete. This can happen either locally, or via a cloud service. TestFairy.com does this for android Beta builds, and sdk.applause.com offers this for both Android and iOS. This approach is likely to spread given its convenience and fewer technical integration issues, and dramatically increase the usage of SDKs.

Overall, the advantages of visibility into your app's performance, and low cost, out of the box SDK solutions, outweigh the disadvantages, but proceed with caution and skepticism.

Tips for App Product Managers

Plan-Do-Check-Act App metrics help you validate your product assumptions, and get clues as to what features and bugs to work on next. If your engagement metrics show that your sign up funnel is losing a lot of folks along the way, consider changing the signup flow. To learn what users might be complaining about in the area of accounts and signup, check your app store reviews. Check if the signup flow is super slow, or pages are failing to load by looking at your New Relic dashboard. Perhaps your app is crashing during sign in—check your crash data on crashlytics.com. If you are debating two signup flow designs, leverage A/B testing metrics to determine which is the best. Check out leanplum.com, and apptimize.com for mobile A/B testing metrics and services. Leverage metrics in everything you do.

KPI's (Key Performance Indicators). At the end of the day, serious apps, and their teams, exist to support a business function. The core goal may be money from app downloads or in-app purchases. The goal may be cost savings for your support team. The goal may be a mobile extension of a brand awareness campaign. Or, the goal may simply be another platform to extend your web or desktop service to where the users are these days. The key in all of this is to understand two things: what are your core business goals, and how does app quality relate and support those goals.

- **Brand Awareness and Marketing** If your app is about brand awareness or marketing, it is important to understand how your company measures awareness, and to track how the mobile app is contributing. Instrument lead generation from the app to other brand properties and campaigns via marketo.com or other marketing and lead measurement services. Compare the cost of your app-specific marketing and development costs to the value it brings to the business. Sometimes, companies just need a mobile app for appearances—that's OK. But, be careful not to deploy a shallow, poor app, that reflects negatively on your brand— watch those app store reviews, and social media via tools such as Salesforce's Radian6.

- **Direct Monetization** If your company lives or dies by sales from downloads or in-app purchases, monitor everything, including your monetization. The app stores provide very basic revenue over time, downloads over time, etc., but they lack deeper analysis such as knowing what ROI you can expect from an ad campaign that gets you into the 20th spot on the top Paid Productivity apps list for example. AppAnnie.com strives to give you a powerful view on how your app is performing monetarily, and how other quality issues, such as reviews, or events such as being featured in the app store, or price changes affect your overall revenue. Burstly.com and Flurry.com provide great analytics on revenue and ad clicking—even supporting their own mobile ad networks for monetization. Also keep an eye for surprise changes in these numbers. If in-app purchases fall off suddenly, it might be that your new app design makes these in-app purchases less discoverable, or perhaps a problem with the app that causes it to fail during the app purchase flow. Keep an eye on these monetization metrics for the most serious of app quality issues, and when you make a change intended to improve monetization, look to see that change reflected in the numbers after you ship.
- **Engagement Platform** If your app monetizes via a subscription service, or the mobile app is viewed as simply an extension of your paid, or advertising-based website, watch those metrics too. Watch for any changes in user activity that might indicate a quality issue, or opportunities to improve your app's quality and design. If fewer users are signing up this week—maybe there are issues with your authentication service, or your app code that talks to Facebook or Twitter during the sign up flows. If you are delivering a video playback service and the number of times users rewind the videos drops to zero—perhaps the rewind button is toast, or missing. Keep an eye on engagement looking for clues to broken functionality, discoverability, or possible design optimizations.
- **Competitive** Benchmark your app against the best. Leverage services like AppAnnie.com, or simply watch the app store data yourself to see how many downloads the

competition is getting. Tools such as the competitive quality radar charts available on analytics.applause.com let you quickly compare your app's quality directly with the averages in your app store category, or see if they are doing better in user-sentiment around quality areas such as performance, privacy, or satisfaction. Maybe your app rocks. Maybe you find a particular quality area difficult such as crashing, but can have some solace that it is also difficult for your competitors' apps as well. Maybe your app needs some TLC in a certain area. Maybe you can spot quality issues where the competition suffers, but where some quality focus on your end can differentiate your app in the market. Much more on competitive analysis later.

- **Cost Savings, Efficiency** Many apps these days are designed for use inside of a corporation. For example, an app for sales reps to play videos and preview your service for potential customers on a tablet with the potential customer. Some teams build apps that let retail store managers take photos of the shelves in disarray, or missing, or mislabeled merchandise to share quickly with staff to resolve the issue. If this is the case for your app, or just an app that you are deploying to solve efficiency issues, measure it. Compare the cost or time with and without the app. Use this data to determine the value the app is delivering.

Granted, most of these metrics and tools provide single windows into the whole of the metrics story. They still fail to automatically relate the quality of your app directly to your monetization or core business goals. A little bit of custom work by exporting the data from these services and throwing them into Business Intelligence tools can be very much worth your time. Appdynamics.com is leading the way, but they are still early and often require quite a bit of customization to pull in all metrics and signals. In the coming years, more apps and services will combine, and auto-analyze and find causal relations between all these quality and monetization signals. Patience is a virtue, but start analyzing your metrics today.

Quality Monster: Competition

"If you know the enemy and know yourself, you need not fear the result of a hundred battles. If you know yourself but not the enemy, for every victory gained you will also suffer a defeat. If you know neither the enemy nor yourself, you will succumb in every battle."
— Sun Tzu, The Art of War

Desktop applications had competition--but the users to find a CD-ROM at a brick and mortar store, or wait for a 25-minute download, and often had to buy it to try it. A web site's competition lives behind a simple blue link in a Google search result. This is closer, but the competition monster is still a few clicks away without pictures. Today's app stores go out of their way to show interested users the competition, with pictures and at the very moment users are deciding whether to download your app. The app world is very competitive with millions of other apps. Literally millions. And, the rich get richer. If you have a good, but not great app, it is unlikely you will be discovered or users will keep you around when the next similar, but prettier app comes by. You have to be brave and honest with your app's quality--compare yourself with the best. Which flappy bird app clone is yours?

Tips for App Testers

App Judo Use your competitor's momentum against them. Although you are likely enamored with your own calendar app, you should be spending more time using the competitive calendar apps. If you aren't aware of what the competitive apps do well, where they fail, what functions they have and don't have, or how easy they are to use, you are probably in for some quality issues of your own. When you are using a calendar for your personal use, perform the same action on all other competitive calendar apps. If you are really ambitious, execute your test plans and test cases on competitive apps to get a great feeling of the holes in your test planning, and how many fewer steps the other app requires for various functions, and the competition's overall quality. Share your competitive quality findings with your development and product manager counterparts—the data could be invaluable to their design, and coding. Testing and using competitive apps is even important before your app's design or test planning is underway. Know the enemy and learn from them.

Watchtower Watch the competition. Watch their star ratings, their feature releases, their app store reviews (good and bad), and blogs where they show off which test automation frameworks they are using. Watch and learn.

Tips for App Developers

Reverse Engineer Look inside the competitions apps. If you aren't shy of command line tools, you can reverse engineer quite a few things about your competition's app. There are quite a few Android APK disassemblers out there that can give you peek into the app's manifest file and other code sections. You can see which 3rd party tools or SDKs they are using. Often you can even tell if they used a cross-compiling tool such as Appcelerator.com, xamarin.com or phonegap.com. Knowing this can help you figure out how they added specific features, or what their engineering limitations they have due to framework selection. There are far fewer tools for iOS IPAs, and it is still much of a secret art, but some of this inspection is still possible. As they say between Saturday morning showings of ThunderCats: "The more you know...".

Copycat If the competition's app can do it, you can do it too. Technically speaking. Look at how other apps deal with app quality issues like poor networking conditions, or user interface (UI) scaling and transitions. If they can deal gracefully with issues that trouble your app's quality, you app can do it gracefully too. Often the most compelling and differentiating features of an app are technically difficult. It is a good thing. Famously, Instagram performed file upload in the background asynchronously to make it feel faster. That wasn't easy. Flipboard built its own JavaScript rendering framework to make every article on the web look great and consistent. They do this because it is hard. Apps are all just ones and zeros at the end of the day, so anything is possible create and clone. There are no excuses if another app can do it.

Tips for App Product Managers

Competitive Grid Follow all the tips for App testers and developers above. Use, copy, reverse engineer, and watch your competitive apps. Do it. If you pretend you don't have competitors in the app stores—you are likely in denial. Build a competitive list detailing features and quality and downloads. Share this list with your testers and developers (not your users) so they can make more informed decisions.

Factory Floor If you are using a vendor for your app development, and you are losing to a competitor with a far better app, consider using that same vendor. If your competitor is building the app in-house, you should consider doing the same. If you know of a great app that you'd like to emulate, or that has the same level of quality and design you are looking for, use the same app development vendor. If the vendor-built app is far superior to your in-house development, consider pricing it out—quietly. Use the best factories possible.

Tester, Developer, PM Tips

Meet and Greet This may sound awkward at first, but there is a strong sense of community, and shared pain and learning in the app world. Your competition is also looking for tips and tricks and sometimes just someone to commiserate with them on their struggles with app quality. They are also quick to brag about how their latest approaches, tooling, and designs have make their apps better. If you are shy, check their blogs. If you are OK with crowds, go to a few app development conferences where the talk in the hallways and the Q&A after talks is often about quality. If you are an A-type personality, reach out to them directly via email or LinkedIn and have coffee. You'll be surprised how much they will share. At the end of the day, everyone wants to be better, faster and have higher quality apps and they can't do it alone.

Quality Monster: User Interface

"As far as the customer is concerned, the interface is the product."
--Jef Raskin

Desktop apps had a mouse and big keyboard and a lot of screen real-estate. Web sites, well, we've always tolerated the clunkiness of web pages, and as you move around the web there are many other sites that look less awesome than yours, so you can feel good about yours. The mobile app world is the worst of all worlds; clumsy thumbs, tiny screens, and most apps try hard to look shiny, and do cool things when users do fancy stuff like pinch, swipe, double tap, etc. Mobile app users also care less about features, they just want something to look great and help them accomplish a task—they don't much care that that own a particular app. App users expect a seamless experience as they move between the OS and your app, and other apps. You can't get away with being too 'odd', out of date, or having a confusing or feature-rich interface. App users expect less functionality and far better user interfaces. UX is often the differentiator in the competitive app store world. Have an awesome UX.

Tips for App Testers

Jack be Quick Are the most common actions in the app available from the home screen? Are there extraneous dialogs, alert messages that get in the way? Anything that slows the user in an app's core user stories is a very bad thing. Does the app require lots of typing, or does it pre-fill suggestions and provide lots of default text for messages like great mobile apps are known to do? Your app's user interface is there to speed up your users, not slow them down.

Tiny Screens Mobile apps mean small screens. Test that buttons are large enough to click, but small enough not to look odd, and separated enough not to click accidentally. Does the app look good on a small phone, as well as a phablet or full-blown tablet? Even the iPad mini has issues with clickable areas on apps that had small buttons to begin with on full-size iPads. Does your app's UI feel crowded with too many buttons? Watch for accidental clicks and never waste screen real-estate.

Gestures What used to be a button, link, or scroll-bar, is now a swipe, a pinch, a tap, or a double tap. Try everything because your users will try them and it could have surprising behaviors. Many UI elements have default behaviors that respond to these inputs, even if the PM or developer didn't think about it, your app might do something. Apps sometimes use these gestures awkwardly—know the expected behavior for these various gestures.

Zebra Does the app look natural in its environment or stand out? Does it fit in with the operating system's interface conventions? If the app deviates from what all the other apps are doing, is this revolutionary new UX, or is it just plain different and confusing? At the end of the day, unless your app's UX is amazingly awesome, much of its UX should have melted away to give pixels to the content or intuitive controls. Blend into your environment, or be noticed for good reason.

Tips for App Developers

Clone vs. Original Code It is tempting to write your own UI components, but it is dangerous. The best apps tend to reuse existing and popular UI libraries—and focus UI innovations on just a few key aspects of their app. Many common controls from the core operating system, and from common UI libraries, have many default behaviors and responses to gestures—you will forget to implement them in your custom controls, and your custom controls are more likely to crash or not behave as the user expects. If you innovate everywhere, it is unlikely that users will have the patience to relearn a new app interface and will fail to discover what makes your app great. Be adventurous in UI if you have the time, technical chops, patience, and it makes sense for your app to differentiate itself. Leave everything else to those who have thought through the design, and tested the controls already. Buy clothes, not sew your own.

Tips for App Product Managers

Clone vs. Original Design It is tempting to come up with a nifty new way to navigate your app, but it is dangerous. A great example of an app that looks great, leverages common UI elements like a toolbar at the top, menu 'hamburger' button, but has a special radial press to reveal options UX is Path. They left the simple stuff simple, and innovated in one key area, and nailed it. Leave everything else to those who have thought through the design issues already. Don't be different for the sake of being different.

Learn from the best It is critical in UX/UI to learn from the best apps out there. Look to the common flows, interactions and controls of the best apps in your app store category. When in doubt, do the same. There are also quite a few books out there on mobile UX design, here are several good ones:

- <u>Android Design Patterns</u> Interaction Design Solutions for Developers, by Greg Nudelman
- <u>Mobile User Experience</u> Patterns to Make Sense of it All, by Adrian Mendoza
- <u>UX Book</u> Process and Guidelines for Ensuring a Quality User Experience, by Rex Hartson and Pardha Pyla

Less is More In general, fewer buttons, fewer required gestures, and a simpler application design is better. Forget the feature wars of the desktop and web past—there is a new war being waged in mobile UX and it is all about simplicity.

Quality Monster: Security and Privacy

"There is no security on this earth; there is only opportunity." -- Douglas MacArthur

With desktop applications, it was widely understood that about any app could read or write any data it likes to your machine. This was a dangerous world, but that's the way it was. Web sites usually posed the threat of leaking the information that you put into them—but only one website at a time. Mobile apps are a bit scarier because the devices they live on can be left on an airplane, or fall out of your pocket at the casino. Your whole digital life is in there. Apps all live next to each other on these devices, and the OS has all your friends phone numbers, and email addresses and selfies. Today's mobile OS's do a pretty good job to save people from apps via sandboxing. But, it is also easier than ever to build an app that does something dorky like log clear text passwords to system, or place private selfies in the camera roll where all the other apps can find it. Some apps are even used to get access to doors in the physical world. An app that asks for more permission that it obviously needs will get slammed. Privacy and security for apps is important, but it is also half perception and half reality--you need to think of both.

Tips for App Testers

Each According to his Need Check for all permissions the app requires. Check the app store description, manifest file, and any

permission prompts that the user sees in a clean app install. If the app asks for permissions that it doesn't obviously need to accomplish its mission, users will be unhappy and vocal. Every year, this issue becomes more prominent. Avoid these issues entirely by asking only for the permissions your app absolutely, and obviously needs. The 'Brightest Flashlight" app was recently found recording the location of 50 million users and selling it to 3rd parties. Don't get into trouble with the Federal Trade Commission (FTC). Don't even look like a bad app. Verify that your app clearly explains why it needs each permission and what it does with the data in privacy documents, app store descriptions, and even in within the app before the app asks the user to grant permissions.

GREP Check everywhere for possible leaks of usernames, passwords, or any personally identifiable information. Check the devices' log files. Search the device's file system. Use a web proxy to search for unencrypted traffic with this data. If you can find it, it is a security issue and privacy leak.

Tips for App Developers

Log Jam Log files are your enemy. Take care that debug logging isn't present in production logs. Double check your #ifdef's around log statements. Take care with what you log or send to 3rd party code or web services: make sure the payload is encrypted, and that you are OK with their retention and security policies.

SSL by Default Apps should use SSL by default in all network calls unless you have an amazingly good reason. Performance is most often a naïve and bad reason to avoid SSL. If the OS has an SSL vulnerability (it happens) it is their fault, not yours and it is unlikely your secure code would have been any better. Don't roll your own.

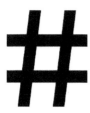

Hashish Haze Before sending data over the network, or saving to the device's local storage, make your best attempt to only persist salted hashes of data where possible. Encrypt and obfuscate data—make your data difficult to use even if it is found.

Tips for App Product Managers

Explain Yourself Tell the user why your app needs every permission. Often users will glance at permissions and walk away if they think you are asking for too much. Explain your permission needs in the app description text, just before the system asks the user to grant permissions, and your privacy policy page. Every app permission request is a chance of losing users who made it far enough to find or install your app.

Over-sharing Posting messages to the user's social accounts showing off their successful install of your app, or wanting to share their new high score every 5 minutes, causes lots of privacy angst for users. Growth hacking in this way is dangerous. Tread carefully.

Quality Monster: Agile Teams

"There is no 'I' in team but there is in win." --Michael Jordan

This monster is you and your team. The exact type of monster depends on your company and how 'app-focused' you are. The rapid shift to app development, and its growing importance in organizations has had some interesting effects on companies, and app quality. You might find yourself in an app startup--where the company lives or dies based on your app's quality. This usually leads to great apps as the entire business is focused, but very dangerous if you ignore the quality monsters. Or, you might find yourself on a team of fellow interns, new hires, or "just another client team", starting to build a mobile companion for the company's web site. This usually leads to useful, but just OK apps as the team isn't as app-focused, or mobile-first. Here, you are in an awesome position if you deliver a great app--you can ride the explosion in mobile and quickly become the most important face of your company in this new app-focused world. You could also find yourself in a company that only sees the app as an extension of your company's brand and marketing, and a vendor might develop it. In this case, it is very important to verify the quality of the app vendor's work, as they aren't always as aligned or aware of your company's goals. Quality reflects on the brand—it is the sole purpose of the app. The world is moving to apps, and particularly mobile apps, so it is imperative to understand your team's weaknesses and strengths related to app quality.

Tips for App Testers

No Time With builds coming out every day, sometimes every hour, app testers can't fully test each build. Accept that reality. Successful testers often do a rolling test regression run where they start on a given build, and move the testing to the next build as soon as it is available until the test pass is complete. They often also run a full set of tests (at least their top priority tests) on release candidate builds.

Listen Listen to user feedback whether it comes from your mom, your CEO, app store reviews or blogs. Pay attention to how many times the same topics are raised as an indicator of importance. Try to understand and reproduce the issues. The most successful and largest app teams often dedicate one or more folks on the team to this task, tracking issues in large spreadsheets, and sharing the data back to the feature teams for inclusion in product planning and bug triage. Listen, and take action. It needs to be someone's job.

Deep Thoughts Quality used to mean functional correctness. Today, app quality spans many areas not traditionally considered by testers. Much more on these quality attributes later.

Tips for App Developers

Backlogs are Dangerous Backlogs cloud your prioritization on quality issues and stunt your creativity. A great work, from one of the original agile folks is called "ReWork" by Jason Fried, and David Heinemeier Hansson. I highly recommend it as a refreshingly agile and lightweight view to all this process that has been heaped upon agile. A great takeaway from ReWork is "Long lists don't get done", so don't have them. Your agile process should be focused on the user, and if they are reporting problems with your app, fix them before you add new features. This simple advice is easy to agree with but difficult to follow. Keep a zero bug backlog.

King Koder In an agile environment, there is less time to bake and test your product. Only check in code that you think is solid. If you don't think it is solid, or your peers don't think it is solid, don't ship it. Only check-in code that is fault tolerant and that you are proud of. If you aren't surprised when you hear of a bug, you aren't checking in solid code in an agile environment. Code like a king if you want to rule the app store.

Sunk Costs The best check-in, especially for agile apps, is to remove a feature or code that just isn't getting used very often. Less code means less bugs. Fewer features often mean a better app. Ignore sunk costs in the interest of having a light, agile code base.

Tips for App Product Managers

Bugs over Features Prioritize bugs and quality over features. This is perhaps the most difficult thing to do in an agile environment where everyone wants to see new user stories implemented. Reward and recognize your team for major quality fixes. When discussing bugs vs. feature triage, come armed with a sense of the impact the bug is having on your users, the applications image and possibly monetary impact. Make bugs personal by quoting app store reviews. It is a sad thing to see so many apps suffer from the same quality issues release after not-so-shiny new release. In the app world, quality debt continues to hammer at your star rating—fix bugs early.

Short Term Thinking If you are planning 3 months ahead or longer, you are probably not agile and not reacting to the fast-moving app market or keeping up with your customers expectations. Be nimble in your planning, as the app stores are full of other apps that are chasing the latest hotness to woo your users away. The OS's are constantly evolving and updating, and your app can quickly look stale. Short-term thinking can be a good thing.

Quality Monster: Reviews

Reviews are a huge monster. Reviews are such a large monster that the remainder of this book is focused on them. Read on.

Section II: Reviews and Stars

In the app world, reviews and star ratings dominate the reality and perception of app quality. Tracking download counts, user engagement, user retention, and monetization via ads or in-app-purchases is also important, but reviews and star ratings impact all of these other key performance indicators. Reviews impact the user's decision whether or not to download the app in the first place.

Interpreting Reviews

Understanding what people are trying to say in their app reviews can be difficult. Sometimes, they will give the app 5 stars while complaining about a bug. Other times, they talk about how their boyfriend left them. It is common to see reviews that mention multiple things, some good, some bad, in the same review, but users are still only able to give the app a single star rating.

App review streams are full of positive, negative, confusing and nutty messages in the review stream for almost every app. Since I'm writing this chapter in a Starbucks, sipping on peppermint mocha, lets look through the Starbucks iOS app reviews for examples of these different types of reviews. Disclosure: I personally love Starbucks lattes, mochas, baristas and even other customers—I'm not picking on them, it is just top of mind.

Reviews can be Positive

Positive reviews are far more common than most app teams realize. Happy users are happy to share what they love about their apps.

Starbucks
Food & Drink | Applause Score: 36...

Review, 5-Star, Starbucks iOS: "Works great for me! Not sure why it's getting bad ratings. It's simple, finds Starbucks for me when I'm on the road, and it stores my info so I don't have carry my Starbucks card. Works like a charm for me, at least." – Wolfywolfywolfy

Review, 5-Star, Starbucks iOS: "I love it! I have had this app since before the Starbucks stores had scanners! Only worked at target in the beginning. I have never in well over two years had an issue! FYI the first review said they lost everything... It's all synced with Starbucks all you need to remember is your sign in! Even Starbucks website says that!" – Scott0030

Reviews can be Negative

App developers and owners are sometimes in denial and avoid the app review stream just like people often ignore negative comments—even when they are constructive or useful. The review streams for apps aren't always the most pleasant things to read. Unhappy users are likely to share the shortcomings of the app—sometimes even the app team itself.

Starbucks
Food & Drink | Applause Score: 36...

Review, 1-Star, Starbucks iOS: "Love Typing Your Password? If you do, get this. You will get to type your password CONSTANTLY! Previous revision remembered the pw, but not any longer. Always nice when a useful feature is removed. Especially in the line at Starbucks when you're trying to move quickly." –Tom in Pheonix

Review, 1-Star, Starbucks iOS: "Won't reload. When reading these reviews I was surprised by how many people have complained that they can't reload their card and the problem has still not been resolved. I am a barista at Starbucks and I hear every day from people about how they cannot reload their card from the app and it is frustrating. I am a user of the app and used to love it but I have gone back to using a gift card since the app that used to be so convenient is no longer is functioning. PLEASE FIX THIS" –frustrated barista

Review, 1-Star, Starbucks iOS: "Please fire the company that made us switch to the new app. I have to reload this app over and over and it keeps failing. This is a great idea of it only worked. Even the manager at my favorite SB said most of her customers quit using it. What's so bad is the company executives apparently dont have a clue or read their own reviews." – Jp4coffee

Review, 1-Star, Starbucks iOS: "No way to give developer app mistakes
Some stores have wrong hours. Some stores are completely in the wrong GPS place. But the kicker -- no way to report these mistakes to Starbucks. Starbucks might want to consider hiring a Yelp app developer." – AStrand

Review, 1-Star, Starbucks iOS: "A joke! Update after update, still having issues with this app. Starbucks needs a new app developer because the one they have has no clue what they're doing." – foreverbfc

Review, 1-Star, Starbucks iOS: "fix things! your message section is THE WORST. I can see I have new messages, can see the preview, but get an error message any time I try to read the message. plus I didn't see a "contact the app developer" link so I had to come back here and post a stupid review instead of sending feedback directly to someone who can work on getting it fixed." – ecole7

Review, 1-Star, Starbucks iOS: "Crashes
This app is junk. Crashes every time. The developer probably wasn't paid well." – Studsar87

Reviews Can Be Clever

Starbucks
 Food & Drink | Applause Score: 36/100

Review, 1-Star, Starbucks iOS: "Details
Like the barista who forgets to leave a little room for cream,
Starbucks has forgotten the iPhone 5's 4" display." – JuiceFive

Reviews can be Nutty

Starbucks
 Food & Drink | Applause Score: 36/100

Review, 3-Star, Starbucks iOS: "My gold card is so ugly. I have
no gripe with this app. It does what it's supposed to do. However,
why is the gold card so ugly? It's uglier than most of my other
standard cards! It make no sense as it is the most difficult to earn!
Please improve." – SigmaSnake

Facebook
 Social | Applause Score: 27/100

Review, 1-Star, Starbucks iOS: "Poor. What a runaround... feel
like a headless chicken... I AN NOT too convinced... yet..." –
Louis E. Jantzen

Tinder
 Lifestyle | Applause Score: 53/100

Review, 1-Star, Tinder, Android: "Awful. Kept resending my
messages about 20 times over making me look completely mental.
Signed out and in and it deleted everything. Thanks Tinder for
emphasizing my already lonely existence!" – Pete Brannan

Representative?

So, the obvious question is whether all these reviews represent the opinion of app users as a whole. No one knows. Flurry, a mobile app analytics company, reported that about 0.5% of users, or 1 in 200 file a review. For those apps that prompt users to file reviews, that number can jump to near 1.5%—more on that below. What we do know is that these users set the tone for your app—they are either your advocates or your detractors, and their input is front and center in the app store at the moment that future users are deciding whether or not to download and try your app. We may never know, because that would mean polling every app user. Regardless, reviewers are an important and vocal minority of users and critical to understand in an app-world.

Further Reading For deeper insight into the distribution of review star ratings, motivations for providing reviews, and positive review bias in general, see: Hu, N., P.A. Pavlou, J. Zhang. 2007. "Why do online product reviews have a J-shaped distribution? Overcoming biases in online word-of-mouth communication". Working Paper. Google it.

Review Statistics

Here are some review statistics to get a feel for the breadth and texture of reviews in the app stores. Below is a chart that shows how many reviews appear in the Lifestyle category. The chart shows how many apps have N reviews. Note that this a LOG chart so the drop off is even more extreme than it looks---very few apps get the majority of all reviews (and downloads).

Distribution of Number of Reviews
Market: Apple, Category: Lifestyle

Review Counts

To date, there are over 200M app reviews posted. The most popular apps have hundreds of reviews coming in each and every day, but most apps have less than 1 review per day.

The number of reviews varies significantly over time. Apps fall out of fashion. Apps also get large influxes of reviews when a new release is amazing or terribly disappoints. Here are some review frequency charts for a few popular apps over a four-month period. Note that that this plot shows the daily count of positive (4 stars or higher reviews) on top, and negative (1 and 2 stars) on the bottom—this gives you a feeling of the trend in overall sentiment as a function of time.

Starbucks
 Food & Drink | Applause Score: 36/100

Can you see the day Starbucks launched its iOS app redesign?

HBO GO
 Entertainment | Applause Score: 30

Can you see the day HBO released Game of Thrones (and their servers went down?)

Facebook
 Social Networking | Applause Score: 43

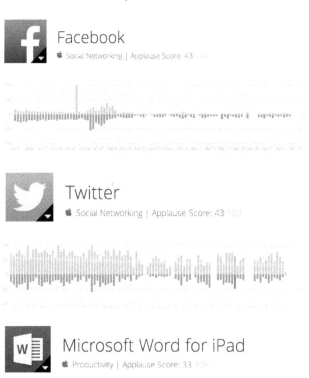

Twitter
 Social Networking | Applause Score: 43

Microsoft Word for iPad
 Productivity | Applause Score: 33

It looks as though Microsoft Word users quickly lost interest.

Interview with Stuart Hall (founder of Appbot.co)

Q: Hi Stuart. I'd love to get your take on App store reviews in general. You are an iOS developer and the founder of Appbot.co— a review monitoring service. What was the genesis of appbot.co?

A: AppBot came about from a pain point I had, keeping up to date with app reviews from all the different stores/countries. Other services existed to let you browse them, but I would never remember so wanted them delivered to me. Initially it was just a simple cron job running on my laptop, then a few others wanted to join, and eventually I built it out to an online service. I've been amazed at the response.

Q: How long have you been building iOS apps?

A: I've been building iOS apps for almost 4.5 years.

Q: What platforms did you develop on before iOS? What are the main differences in your between developing an app for a platform with and without an App store with Review feedback?

A: I've moved through the entire stack, I initially started my career developing devices drivers and embedded systems, then some C on Solaris real-time systems, then moved into some C++, then onto .NET, then Ruby on Rails and now iOS development.

Q: What do you wish the app store reviews had that they don't today? Do you wish they had the ability to contact the person who filed the feedback? Or wish they had richer 'bug filing' and separate tracking software? Or that they had more information on the user or their device?

A: More information about the user and devices would be great to help diagnose problems, but I can't see Apple adding this any time soon.

Q: App store reviews sound like a great source for feedback and connection with your user base, but not everyone files reviews. Do the reviews represent the voice of all your users, or just the most vocal users? How does that impact how reviews should be interpreted and prioritized for an app developer?

A: It's definitely from the two extremes, people need a strong reaction (good or bad) to take the time to go and leave a review. This is why I think it's so important to read them. That person who has taken 5 minutes out of their day to go and complain about your app is someone that you need to listen to.

Q: Have you noticed any difference between the reviews in the Google Play store versus the Apple App Store? If so, what differences? If not, why do you think the app stores and their users are very similar?

A: Can't really answer this one, haven't done any Android apps and AppBot doesn't support Google Play yet.

Q: Are you seeing an increase or decrease in interest and demand from app developers to read and respond to their app store reviews?

A: Definitely seeing an increase as app development has become more professional and teams have grown.

Q: How do you deal with Reviews from different countries—do you notice any differences in the types of things mentioned in reviews from country to country?

A: I see the same things mentioned in reviews over and over. Translations are obviously an issue to non-English speaking countries.

Q: For large apps, there are hundreds of reviews that come in each day— any advice to developers on how to handle that much data?

A: From the AppBot customers the large apps seem to have product and support guys whose job is to deal with it.

Q: Many developers seem to shy away from the app store reviews because it can hurt to see people saying bad things about the app you spent so much time on. Any thoughts on that?

A: I was like that originally as well, but I think this sort of unsolicited feedback is extremely valuable. Now I see negative app reviews as motivation to improve my apps.

Q: How do you get feedback on your own apps before you ship?

A: I like to ship early and get feedback from real users as fast as possible.

Q: (totally optional, folks will be curious and might be a way to show off your growth if u are interested) How many developers use Appbot.co? How many apps do you monitor?

A: Currently there are 4200 developers tracking over 22,000 apps. Growth has been strong. Here is a chart of the number of apps tracked since launch:

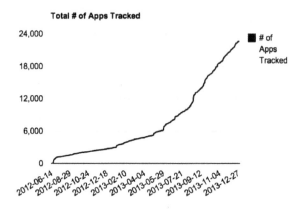

Total # of Apps Tracked

Q: Wow, that sounds like you are having an impact on the teams that build the apps I use every day! Just curious, how much of your time does Appbot.co take? Did you build it by yourself? Are you working 24/7 on this, or does it run on its own now?

A: AppBot is something I have just built in my spare time, I've spent an average of 1 hour a week on it since launch. I plan to spend more time on it over the coming months.

Q: That sounds like a lot of work for you. Technically, how are you able to crawl all these reviews? Can you share some of your basic technology with the other nerds out there, or share insight into the toughest engineering problem you faced building Appbot.co?

A: I think like most businesses and services the engineering is the easy part, building a brand and finding customers is always more difficult.

Q: Any general advice to app developers on handling review feedback, positive or negative?

A: Don't take it personally, look at it as a great way to get feedback and improve your apps.

Q: Do you think it is useful, or distracting, to look at the reviews of competitive apps?

A: It's not something I do a lot myself, but many AppBot customers do, especially the larger developers. I can see it being a great way to see weaknesses in competitor's apps, but also a big distraction.

Q: Are there any specific reviews that you thought were funny, or particularly interesting off hand? Anyone can write a review, so I image there are some good ones!

A: There are always some really great ones coming through, here is one I had for one of my apps that makes me laugh every time I see it

Review, 5-Star: "Great Sandwich. I was eating a real good sandwich when I came across this app, and was amazed " – Michael Johnson

Q: What is next for you and Appbot.co?

A: I'm in the process of adding Google Play support, and then I have (what I think is) some very exciting pro features coming.

Q: In closing, I'd love to say thanks for building an awesome and simple to use service for app store review monitoring.

A: Thank you!

Spam

The question of review spam often comes up. There are fears of international 'farms' of workers blindly adding hundreds of positive reviews for products. This may happen to a degree—especially from friends and family of the developers themselves, but overall it looks that the law of large numbers and the anti-spam work of the app stores is doing a great job. Note that both Google Play and Apple's App Store don't allow posting ratings or reviews for apps that users have not purchased or downloaded. These stores also now require users to be authenticated with an account. It is interesting that across 100 million plus reviews analyzed, very few reviewers have made more than a 100 reviews, and none have made more than the magic number of a 1000 reviews. When looking at the reviews posted by the folks with many hundreds of reviews, they read as pretty legit, not 'review farming'—they seem to be made by very, um, retentive people, and/or people that are trying to build up Yelp-like credibility in the app review world. Also keep in mind that many real-world users, like myself, have installed (and uninstalled) hundreds of apps. All this points to review spam not being a major problem.

Apps with No Reviews

A surprisingly large number of apps in the app store have zero reviews. On the order of two-thirds of all apps in the app stores have no reviews. What is most interesting about this stat is that it means the developers themselves, and none of their friends or family even bothered to rate the app. Sad. This implies many of the apps in the app stores are small experiments, or 'testing', perhaps never meant to be discovered.

Actively Reviewed Apps

The app stores are literally full of over a million apps each, but there are a surprisingly small number of apps that have new reviews coming in during any given month. This might be a proxy for the apps users are actually using. For both Google Play and the Apple App Store, only about 50,000 apps have new reviews coming in for them each month. The rest of the apps appear dormant...or users have chosen not to review them ever again.

Prompting

A special note belongs here about prompting users for review feedback. You might have noticed this happening in your own app usage. It is a clever idea really. The app prompts the user for feedback by asking, "do you love the app?", or "are you frustrated?". If the user loves the app, they are whisked immediately to the app store to share their appreciation for the app. If the user indicates that they are frustrated with the app, the app says sorry and asks the user to share their feelings privately with the app owner.

Apptentive.com is a startup that automates much of this process for app developers. Here is a screenshot of the basic app flow:

The Good

There is quite a bit of goodness here. First of all, given the importance of app store star ratings, the app developers often can see a bump of close to half a star rating or so. Really. That sounds good, even though it might feel a little bit like gaming the system. The applause.com team noticed twitter started prompting users for reviews in this manner, and predicted they'd see about a half point of star rating improvement in the coming weeks—it happened.

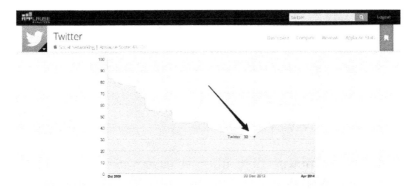

Users who are frustrated get to tell the developer directly. The user might not have shared their feelings publicly unless prompted, so the app owner gets more data with wish to make a better app, and perhaps a save an engaged user. Most importantly though, the app owner can capture the user's email address, so they can write back to the user with more questions on the issue or to personally let the user know the issue has been resolved. This direct channel of communication between the app developer and the user is a great thing.

The Not So Good

All the goodness explained, there is another side to prompting users for feedback:

- It somewhat undermines and distorts the public review data for an app. Filling it with a few more happy reviews, and blocking some negativity from the public view.
- It almost always causes public review blowback, with users complaining about their user experience being interrupted by an apparently self-serving prompt for feedback. App users appear particularly sensitive to interrupting their flow, versus traditional web and desktop apps as their time in the app is limited. That said, the positive impact to an app's ratings often outweigh any backlash.

Google Maps
 Navigation | Applause Score: 72/100

Review, 1-Star, Google Maps iOS: "1 star for bugging me to review. " –username12345

Review, 1-Star Google Maps, iOS: "They asked for a review. So I gave them one." –Dave Weatbrook

- Several prominent app companies have rolled out similar functionality, but realized the cost/benefit was low, and removed this prompting. It is too early to know of this is a trend but it is worth noting.

Quick Interview with Robi Ganguly, the co-founder of Apptentive:

Q: Hi Robi, Can you please share a quick overview of Apptentive's mission? ...and how the Apptentive service works as a solution to that mission?

A: Sure - we exist to help companies talk with their customers. We believe that companies should be striving to earn the love of their customers and that in order to do so, they must communicate with them in a more personal manner.

Our service is super focused on the connection between mobile app customers and the publishers of those apps. We give mobile app publishers tools to power communications, inside their apps, in order to increase customer satisfaction, improve customer retention and really increase the feedback loop.

Q: So, Apptentive is focused on building the relationship between the app and the user. How do app teams typically incorporate user feedback into their product development lifecycle?

A: Teams typically look at user feedback as helpful in a few ways: 1) Prioritization 2) Satisfaction measurement 3) Acceptance testing.

I'll break that down a bit. First, most product management organizations struggle with prioritization, so when teams work with us, they typically find that they hear from a LOT more customers and get a much better sense of the places where the most friction and frustration is occurring. As a result, we hear from many teams who say their product management roadmap is now 60%+ derived from direct customer conversations and insights. This happens not just because of the feedback, but also because everyone on the team gets added to the Apptentive inbox, enabling more of the company's stakeholders to really be in the flow of information from customers.

Second, one of the measurements that matters more than ever before for software these days is customer satisfaction. App teams use us to get a daily measurement of customer happiness and, over time, establish a benchmark of happiness for each version of their app. As a result, there's a very clear metric for the mobile team to determine if they're making their app better or not.

Finally, when teams roll out new features, they often don't know how the new features are received and if they make sense to consumers. When companies work with us, they'll often set up a survey after a new feature is used, in order to ask a few questions about how the feature landed and how it could be improved. As a result, new features that are released out into the wild are opportunities for immediate feedback.

Q: Can you share a concrete example of feedback impacting a real-world app team?

A: Sure, we hear about lots of them all the time. Here's a recent one that comes to mind that was particularly powerful and simple at the same time. One of our customers redesigned their app to try and address some issues with onboarding that they were seeing. In the redesign, they introduced a "splash page" as the first screen customers would see when opening the app. Shortly after releasing the new app, the team started to receive a large number of "the app doesn't work, why is there just one screen?" comments through Apptentive. In responding to those customers and examining what they meant, they found that the splash screen, which could be removed with a swipe, wasn't very intuitive to many of their consumers. So, they added a visual sign that the splash screens could be swiped, which addressed all of the customer confusion.

Q: Do you track the impact of making a single user happier? Does it spread happiness on the web and in the App Store, or is it just one user at a time? How do you measure that impact?

A: We do track some of the impacts of having happy customers. For starters, happy customers of mobile apps stick around longer. We all know that retention is a massive problem for mobile apps (>90% of consumers who download an app are gone within 6 months) so it's important to figure out what makes people happy. Secondly, when you know that a customer is happy, you can ask them to take actions to share their experience with others - from the app store to the real world. We measure app store ratings and reviews, the sentiment expressed in those reviews and the overall happiness indicators we have inside of apps in order to quantify customer happiness for our customers. Our tools help mobile teams manage this process at scale, so for each consumer it feels very individualized but the rollout and execution is actually happening across the entire app's audience.

Q: Apptentive has lots of data and experience with what types of things make users love an app--can you share a few?

A: Here are some keys to ensuring that your app is loved:

- Simple and straightforward design around core use cases. Apps that try to accomplish too much too quickly or that try to jam all of the company's web features into an app often result in customers feeling confused and frustrated.

- Iterating quickly. When apps are updated and changes are rolled out on a regular basis, customers feel like the app is living, which leads to a more ongoing relationship and discovery.

- Listening to customer input. In the early days of every app, the app is in search of use cases that are really core to the audience. By listening to the early fans, mobile teams can determine what is important and useful to their fans, which enables them to invest further in the areas that matter most to a customer.

- Communicating with customers. Most of us establish emotional relationships with the people who work at companies, not the company itself. By communicating with an app's mobile customers companies are able to create relationships and emotional connections with the end consumer, increasing loyalty and personal connection.

Q: Why do customers fall out of love with an app?

A: Consumers often fall out of love with an app that they previously loved because it's changed in a meaningful way that has hindered their use of it. Sometimes this is because the app is crashing in numerous places or in a significant flow. Other times it's because the app decided to expand in a significant way that left the core usage behavior behind. When you get used to using an app in a certain way and then you open it up only to find that the entire app is working differently, this can really push you away. Finally, if an app is wonderful and adored, but doesn't get updated every 2 or 3 months, at a minimum, many consumers are likely to get bored and go looking for apps that have more consistent upgrade patterns.

Q: How to app teams avoid information overload when they start getting feedback or real time chats from so many users?

A: For many teams, there isn't much of an information overload problem in the early days. When your app is small and not a whole lot of people are using it, Apptentive allows you to communicate and connect with a large % of your customer base. As your audience grows, you can use our tools, like surveys, to create methods for structuring and understanding what consumers care about at scale. In addition, because our inbox is designed for multiple people within an organization by inviting more of your colleagues into our inbox you can share the work of reading, analyzing and acting upon customer input. We routinely find that our customers will add 10 to 25 people from their teams to the inbox so that more people are aware of what's going on and to connect with customers.

Q: We sometimes see reviews saying 'don't bug me for an app review' :-) It seems prompting users for feedback or reviews results in great data, and even better star ratings overall, but can you talk to that? How does Apptentive enable smarter prompting for user feedback?

A: Sure - we see this a lot more these days as well. This is a result of developers using open source ratings prompts libraries that just focus on getting customers to the app store to rate the app. From the first day we had a version of a ratings prompt, we've been focused on making it more about the end consumer. In our view, the right way to approach this problem is to figure out when consumers have had "moments of success" and when they've reached "moments of completion". If you can find a customer who has been successful and who has completed their task, that's a good opportunity to reach out and figure out how the consumer is feeling. IF that customer is delighted, only then is it ok to ask them if they'd be open to rating the app - the rest of the customers are better suited to giving you feedback and helping you make the app better.

In addition, if you're investing in ratings prompts but not collecting any data on the interactions, you're doing it wrong. It's absolutely crucial that you understand how the interactions are going and that you have the tools to make changes to your settings on the fly. Hard-coding these settings and not learning from how customers are interacting with your prompts is a recipe for disaster.

Q: What is the Love Score? How could an app developer use that competitively?

A: The Love Score is an Apptentive-produced score based upon various factors in the app stores, from ratings and reviews to reviewer trends and the ratio of happy to frustrated customers. In addition, we are able to calibrate these trends against what we see internally at Apptentive, based upon our work with thousands of app publishers. Ultimately, it's a measure of how happy an app's customer base is and it can be used to measure both your app and your competitors' apps. We're in the early days of mobile apps and our customers have been clamoring for better metrics and methods of evaluating how their apps resonate with customers - this is our answer. Companies with great Love Scores can feel confident that they're on the right path and companies who have work to do on their Love Score should know they're not the only ones who are struggling. They can come work with Apptentive to improve their Love Score today :)

Q: Any tips for folks that produce surveys? What types of questions are useful and which aren't when surveying mobile users?

A: We see a lot more companies running surveys in mobile these days and we've found that there are some very specific guidelines:

- When you show the survey is crucial. Don't display it in the midst of a task - your completion rates will be horrendous and you'll ultimately end up losing some customers because they've been interrupted.

- Tapable, quick to answer questions are particularly useful in the mobile context, because people are used to a tap-based interface. More complicated input methods don't tend to do well.

- In general, surveys with 3 questions or less do the best.

Q: What is different about relationship management on mobile versus the web or desktop software? What is better? What is more difficult?

A: On mobile devices, most of the time you can assume that there is one person per device (note that this isn't the same for tablets). As a result, relationship management on mobile can be much more frictionless - because you can assume that a single person is using the device you can start to have dialogs with the consumer without requiring logins, email addresses etc. In our tools, for example, we power an in-app inbox that doesn't require a whole lot of identification from the consumer in order to kick off the process of conversing.

However, because mobile is a much more personal environment with a consumer base that has higher expectations, it's challenging for desktop and web-based companies to make the transition. The consumer expects higher touch services, with more listening and conversing. Companies that expect to deliver the same level of service as they do on their website are often surprised to find that mobile consumers are much more vocal and are more likely to be frustrated by not hearing back from a company. The app store's ratings and reviews mechanisms, for example, don't exist on the desktop and web for most apps, so this new channel for customer conversation presents a big challenge.

Q: Where do you see this world moving? What does feedback, and the analysis of user feedback look like in 2017?

A: I think by 2017, we'll see that most digital companies have really become mobile-oriented companies, meaning that they'll start with the mobile experience for a consumer and work from there. That means, given the changing nature of the customer's expectations, that they'll all have to listen to customer feedback and make sense of it, acting quickly to incorporate and learn from it. More importantly, we see consumers continuing to increase their pace of sharing their opinions, leading to an explosion in customer conversations and the creation of feedback. Every company in the space will need to have a strategy in place not just for the aggregation and analysis of the feedback, but also direct communication, at scale, with their customers at the right time and right place.

Q: If you could give app teams one piece of advice (other than using Apptentive!), what would it be?

A: I think everyone in the app ecosystem needs to view the act of creating an app as an ongoing process. For the past few years, too many companies have thought of an app as a "checkbox" - a task that could be finished and moved on from. This is a mistake. Every app can constantly get better and investing in making a mobile app means that you should have an eye towards that ongoing investment and activity from day one.

Review Clustering

As app developers are discovering how important their star ratings and app reviews are to their agile and lean processes, many are starting to formally manage reviews within their companies. Some of the larger app teams even have dedicated 'Customer Feedback' teams. I've met quite a few of them in the course of my work at uTest.com/Applause.com. The customer advocate's job is to read all sorts of feedback from the app stores and social media, and provide feedback to the app development team on what to fix, add or remove next.

The state of the art today is often someone copy/pasting reviews off of the app stores and into a spreadsheet. uTest.com even sells this as a manual service. For popular apps, the job often boils down to grouping similar reviews together and counting how frequently they occur, to approximate how big of an issue it is. The analytics.applause.com team realized this is a huge time sync, often error-prone, and worked to automate the grouping and prioritization of reviews. The automation the team used is a variant of k-means clustering (http://en.wikipedia.org/wiki/K-means_clustering).

Here are some examples of auto-generated output for some popular apps, which goes to demonstrate that the users are talking, and many are saying the same things, and it pays to address their issues. Note that each 'cluster' shows the number of similar reviews, the average star rating for all these reviews combined, and the range of dates where this comment occurred. It's a much more efficient way to get high-level view of the app review feedback for top app teams, versus combing through thousands of reviews manually. There is a lot of great data in reviews if you are looking.

Review Cluster, 1.65-Star, Count 100, 1/13-2/25, Facebook, iOS: "My Video Album on Facebook has tons of videos uploaded via PC, but I can't see them…"

Review Cluster, 1.73-Star, Count 51, 1/29-4/2, Facebook, iOS: "after 5 minutes on the home screen it logs me out…"

Review Cluster, 1.85-Star, Count 100, 1/14-3/15, Netflix, iOS: "My app worked fine until I did the update on my iPhone. Now when I try to play from my iPhone it just keeps crashing .."

Review Cluster, 1.85-Star, Count 6, 3/23-3/30, Netflix, iOS:
"When you chose a genre, it lists the exact same movies/tv shows every time, for every genre…"

Review Cluster, 2.75-Star, Count 4, 2/22-2/24, Netflix, iOS:
"Wow lots of bad reviews…but other than a few annoying bugs It is pretty Good…"

Review Cluster, 2.87-Star, Count 13, 12/31-3/21, Netflix, iOS:
"I switch to my account but it keeps showing movies for my kids account.."

You can see from a quick look at top review clusters that many users are complaining about the same top issues, and they are having a huge impact on the overall star rating. They also sound very fixable. Agile teams should be watching these reports and fix them quickly, especially when they see many of the same issues reported over and over again.

It might not be obvious, but you can also tell from these clusters, if issues have been fixed. If a specific issue was reported 10 times a day for 3 days, and then never again, that might be the sign of a server fix, or that new client build actually resolved the issue leading to happier customers and a higher star rating. Auto bug verification via end-user app store reviews—which is the perfect form of fix validation.

It is also worth pointing out that you can measure the ultimate 'star value' of a given issue when you cluster them like this. This data can be helpful in deciding how relatively, and absolutely, important a given cluster is to your app's quality. It might be better to fix an issue reported only 10 times, but with an average star rating of 1 star, versus something reported 20 times, but with a 2.5 average star rating. This will likely be missed, but this is pretty amazing—we can actually quantify the relative impact of a bug on the user based on these metrics. Pre-app stores, this was only an educated, and often biased and incorrect guess as to severity and priority. Thanks to the app stores, we have additional data to drive our bug triage and feature prioritization.

App Quality: Secrets for Agile App Teams

Quality Attributes and Signals

Attributes

In the summer of 2012, the applause team spent a fair amount of time reading through thousands of app store reviews—trying to discern if there were any patterns. I wanted to see if there was any signal in the noise. We soon discovered that most, about 70% of all reviews, fell into one of ten common flavors of reviews:

- **Content** relevance of an app's data or content across locations and cultures
- **Elegance** how attractive, cool or slick an app's design is
- **Interoperability** how well an app integrates with other services or hardware
- **Performance** how fast and responsive an app is
- **Pricing** how an app's perceived value compares with its cost
- **Privacy** comfort with an app's terms of service and handling of personally identifiable information (PII)
- **Satisfaction** how well an app satisfies users' core expectations
- **Security** functional ease, or perceived risk to sign ins, passwords or other sensitive information
- **Stability** how often the app crashes, hangs or freezes
- **Usability** ease of navigation and discoverability among an app's features

This was pretty cool news. We weren't sure what to expect, but it turns out that the masses of people filing reviews were saying about the same things about most apps—there was hope we could make use of this data. Given that our little team was full of ex-Google and ex-Bing engineers, we of course had to crawl all app store reviews. To date, the team has crawled 200,000,000+ reviews across iOS and Android using about 1000 machines in Amazon's EC2. We then set the data engineers loose.

It turned out to be more complicated than we were expecting:

- Many reviews talk about several issues at the same time, and the star rating for each review only applied to the whole review.
- There are many misspellings, and slang.
- Not every mention of "crash" is an application crash.

Signals

The team then spent a fair amount of human and computer time to see what words were most frequently associated with each quality attribute. The words most commonly used for each category looked pretty reasonable. These are called **quality signals**. For each attribute we found the set of words that highly correlated with a review ending up in one of the quality attributes. This was an exhausting process, and included a fair amount of work just to eliminate words that appeared in more than one attribute. We also had to take care of plural, past tense, etc., versions of each word. Including misspellings that happen often on mobile keyboards. Some obvious signal words were also excluded as they often caused false-positives.

The team also evaluated other methods to classify reviews. Most state of the art sentiment analysis algorithms broke down on the shortness of the review text, misspellings, and relative density of confusing words. For example, most sentiment analysis techniques showed that people were very upset about the Angry Birds app, because most of the reviews contained the word "Angry". The team also looked to use machine learning, so leveraged the uTest crowd to classify reviews into one of these 10 buckets. But, it turns out that humans only have about a 60% chance of agreeing on any given review classification—so we stopped short of trying to train a bank of neural network classifiers, as it would just be noise. Ultimately, the signal-word method used today also has the advantage that when it fails, it is easy to tell why it failed.

We'll explore the quality signals for each attribute in detail below.

Most Chatty Quality Issues

The app store is full of reviews. What are people talking about most? Across the app store, this is the breakdown of how often users are talking about different things—for good and for bad. The larger the bar, the more often folks are talking about that specific quality attribute:

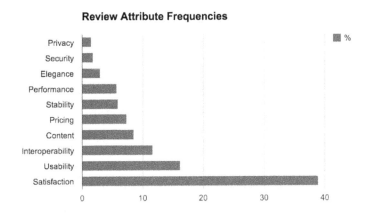

Lets walk through each app quality attribute in turn. For each attribute we will discuss one or more of the following:

- **Attribute Definition:** quick description of this attribute
- **Technical Context:** what technically causes these types of issues
- **Human Context:** how do people contribute to these types of issues

- **Review Signals:** words in reviews that indicate a quality issue of this type
- **App-Specific Sources:** what app-specific issues contribute to these issues
- **Example Reviews:** reviews typical of this quality attribute
- **What can app Testers do?** actionable tips for app testers
- **What can app Developers do?** actionable tips for app developers
- **What can app Product Managers/Owners do?** actionable tips for app PMs
- **Exemplar Apps**: apps that demonstrate perfection is possible for this quality attribute
- **Tools and Services:** a sample of tools or services to help in this area.

Quality Attribute: Stability

"Sometimes we crash and burn. It's better to do it in private."
--Dean Kamen

Attribute Definition:

Apps crash, hang and freeze all the time. It is annoying, and worse—your users will leave you when it happens.

We've all experienced using an app and then it suddenly disappears on iOS, or you see the ugly 'force close' dialog on Android. Apps aren't all that stable compared to their web and desktop cousins. Apps are often seen crashing, freezing and hanging. On iOS when applications crash, the app often will simply disappear and the user will be dropped back to their home screen—this causes confusion, sometimes causes data-loss. And this always causes a bit of anxiety in users. Stability is one of the most solvable issues with mobile apps.

Technical Context

- **Mobile apps simply have far less memory available to them than their desktop cousins.** The amount of memory isn't fixed either. It depends on many variables: device model, age of operating system version, other applications running in background, system operations, and the rumor is that gamma rays are also involved.
- **Apps are 2nd tier citizens on mobile devices** On the desktop, apps can often take over the entire machine's resources if they like. Mobile apps don't fully own their lifecycle. On mobile, the operating system aggressively

protects core features from large or poorly written applications, so if the phone is running low on memory, it sometimes sends memory warnings to apps, then starts zapping them.

- **Mobile Networking is Fragile.** Mobile devices are often connected to networks via 3G, LTE, WIFI, or Bluetooth connections. Not only are these networks far less reliable (and slower) compared to desktop or server LAN connections, but mobile users are also on the go and the phones automatically switch between these networks automatically. All this leads to a far less reliable network than users and developers are used to depending on. Apps are far more likely to enter non-stable states due to networking issues than desktop apps or web pages. Apps that assume a network connection is always there, always reliable and always fast are the some of the most vulnerable to crashing. If your app depends on any network connectivity, never trust that it is there and handle every possible error condition gracefully.
- **Fragmentation in Capabilities** Phones, tablets, even "phablets", have a wide variety of device capabilities. Often the testing is done on a current high-end device, or a simulator or emulator running on a desktop machine. What happens when your memory intensive app works great on a Nexus 5 with a 10MP today, you ship your app, and next week a new Samsung comes out with a 40MP camera? Crash. Boom. You load the image into memory, and this pushes your app over the limit and the OS shuts you down while trying to add an antique filter to a photo of your dog.
- **Device Capabilities** Often Developers will write code that expects a certain number of features to be present on all phones—which is a dangerous gamble. This is particularly an issue for Android developers. It's often overlooked that many devices are missing what may seem like basic features. This will only get worse, as low-price devices ship in the developing world where shaving a few bells and whistles off the hardware can drop the price just enough that millions more can afford access to the devices. As we move toward the 'internet of things', where devices may be

smaller than a penny, and have only basic input and output, this will only get worse. Developers cannot make many assumptions about the capabilities of the device on which their app will run—and it is best to update the manifest, or iOS build requirements to ensure the app is only stalled on devices that can support it. If those features are necessary for the application's basic functionality it is best to avoid installation on these devices in the first place. Android developers should check out: http://developer.android.com/guide/topics/manifest/uses-feature-element.html. iOS Developers should be sure to target the right iOS versions.

Human Context

- **Many mobile developers are new to native app development**. They often come from web development backgrounds. This means that developers are learning new programming languages while they are building the app. Objective-C (iOS) and Java (Android) are far less forgiving than HTML/JavaScript environments—they often crash the application by default when unexpected or unhandled exceptions happen. JavaScript would just keep marching on silently. Mobile app developers are often in more of a rush to get their app completed and into the app store, which only adds to the risk.
- **Too little app testing is looking for crashes**. Developers and testers often spend much of their time validating the expected behavior of the app: "click this, make sure that happened". They often ignore the causes of crashes: network failure. Low-memory due to other applications, and unexpected input. Testing efforts should be targeted at flushing these issues out into the open.
- **Fixing crashes isn't glamorous or fun**. It may seem odd, but even the best funded and brightest developers know about many of the crashes in their applications (including 'stack traces' and device state), but they either have difficulty reproducing these issues in their lab, or more often than not, they are simply overly focused on adding

the next new feature to their app instead of fixing crashes. For too many companies, and developers, fixing a crash just isn't as valuable as adding a feature.

Review Signals

If a review contains some or all of these words, it is often related to the Stability quality attribute:

- access
- crash
- downtime
- froze/frozen
- hang

App-Specific Sources

These are app-specific issues that strongly impact the stability quality attribute:

- **Mobile Networks**: mobile networks are extremely unreliable compared to their laptop and desktop cousins, and can appear and disappear from the app's perspective at any time. These networks have different capabilities, different firewall and traffic filtering rules, and varying speeds, and different cost structures.
- **Device Fragmentation** Especially in the Android world, there is a high variety in available memory, OS limits, and device capabilities.
- **Device State**: The device itself may be fresh from the store with only a few apps. More often however, the device is a swamp of apps, full file systems, custom launchers etc. Usually, there are many other apps running, low battery, and peripherals like headphones and HDMI cables plugged and unplugged at whim. Users toggle permissions (like access to email, contacts, notifications, etc.) outside of the app even while the app is running. Expect the unexpected.
- **Web vs. Hybrid vs. Native vs. Other** Some apps are HTML web apps written for the mobile browser. Some are

Native apps, written for the platform directly. And others are Hybrid apps that are native apps that contain a web app, or a few web pages inside them. Web and Hybrid apps are far less likely to crash than native apps, as JavaScript 'crashes' don't often cause failure of the entire app—only portions of functionality will degrade if there are programming errors. Unhandled exceptions in native apps, where the programming environment is far less forgiving, are the cause of most app crashes. Then there are the "others". There are other 'app types' like phone-gap or appcelerator.com generated apps where the app is written in HTML/JavaScript, but makes calls outside the browser and into native phone features—these apps are often less crashy than native, and more crashy than pure web apps. Your apps design will significantly impact its level of crashing.

- **Location** Knowing the users location is critical for many modern apps. Location data can also be the cause of many application crashes. Apps that ask a server for information relevant to the current location can often return zero results if the location is off the beaten path—when the app expects to always have data for every location, this can cause crashes or bad behavior in the app code. Mobile operating systems can also automatically ping the application when the user's location changes. If these updates come at an unexpected time, while the app is busy handling a previous location update or doing other work, this can cause threading or other stability issues. Apps often expect to always have access to location data after initial app install, but the user can turn this off via the OS settings later, causing crashes if the app code doesn't always check whether it has access.

- **User Experience** It is best if the application handles most crashes itself, whenever possible. It looks pretty awful to the user if the crashes and freezes are announced by the operating system via cryptic dialogs or if the application just disappears altogether. When the app crashes, users are often legitimately concerned that they might have lost the data they were in the middle of working on. Detecting crashes, handling it quietly, and bringing the user back to what they were working on originally should be basic expectations. An apology dialog when things are unrecoverable also goes a long way.

- **Responsiveness** If your app does long winded calculations, or waits forever for the server to respond, mobile operating systems will think something is wrong and quickly bring up a dialog that says 'I think the app has gone wonky'. It is important for apps to never block their main thread of execution—the mobile OS is watching and will crash your app.
- **Distribution** App distribution brings a few nuances for stability issues. The iOS app store doesn't let developers instantly update their app with crash fixes. You can call them and beg for an accelerated review process, but it typically takes about a week to get your new build with your bug and crash fixes pushed out to users. This means it is very important to test for crashes before you push your first app to the app store. An app team's first week in the app store is often spent watching the reviews pile up with reports of crashes and unhappy users. On Android, you can update your app with fixes quickly, but your app can be distributed to many devices you've never heard of or dreamed of---or tested. For Android, it is imperative to restrict the distribution of your app to the OS versions and devices with the capabilities your app expects, or your app will likely crash horribly on a variety of devices.

Version 1.0.1 Posted Aug 3, 2013
Fixes for the top few bugs/crashes from our first release.

Version 1.0 Posted Jul 23, 2013
This is our first public release.

Version 0.9 Posted May 16, 2013

Figure: Quip's iOS release notes. Crash fixes about one-two weeks after launch, as is typical.

Example Reviews:

Fixing crashes can make users happier--and they even crow about it:

Flipboard: Your Social News Magazine
News | Applause Score: 84/100

Review, 5-Star, Flipboard, Android: "Perfect. This is an awesome app. It always works great! I haven't had one crash yet. Love it..." – JessicatP

Instagram
Social | Applause Score: 71/100

Review, 5-Star, Instagram, Android: "Happy ;) Woohoo Finally This Crash prob. Solved !! 5 STARS for this" – Nisarg Naik

Crashes and Freezes make for sad users.

Snapchat
Social | Applause Score: 45/100

Review, 1-Star, Snapchat, Android: "Terrible app. It will freeze up whenever I open it and the camera never opens.....worst app ever downloaded!" –Emma Heminger

Podcasts
Entertainment | Applause Score: 14/100

Review, 1-Star, Apple Podcasts, iOS: "Behaves like an alpha! I use the podcast app more than most apps on my iPhone 4S. Since updating to iOS7, I routinely am forced to do a hard reset or wait for a crash and restart cycle after launching this app! Please resolve! If the app is not ready for release, do not release. I expect a functional and polished product from Apple." – Imiyashiro

Tips for App Testers

The folks that test apps love crashes the best. There is very little debate as to whether a crash is a bad thing, and if they grab the crash logs (see nerd notes below), they can give the developers a lot of information as to what part of the application crashed. Take some tips from the top crowd testers on how to find crashes in apps.

Top Crash Test Cases

Unplug Try app functionality, especially functionality that is network dependent, while messing with the network. Network states to test: slow, on/off, public Wi-Fi, switch between LTE, 3G and Wi-Fi. Turn the network on/off at unexpected times in the middle of app usage or just before and after launching the app. Often applications will assume the network is still there when it isn't. A very common place where apps crash or get stuck due to networking issues is when the user signs-in/authenticates, and when apps are actively streaming audio, video or downloading a file--they don't like the network to change on them. Also, try using the app on a Starbucks or other public network--before you have accepted the terms on the landing page for that router/network. That is an in-between state where there is technically network access, but the DNS points to the signup page.

Dizzy Testers should flip the app between landscape/portrait. Yeah, just flip the device and watch as it tries to rotate through many different UI states. If the app is a game that you can control via tilting the device, then tilt away. Spin the device along all axes. Many apps will eventually crash under this pressure. The more complex the UI, the more likely the app is to crash.

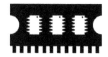

Memento Test the app under low memory conditions. Use older devices, lots of apps running, and load up hundreds of pictures, music, or videos into the app—as many as you can. Create as many new documents as possible. If your app displays contacts, load ten thousand contacts into your device, and then see how your app does browsing this monster list. Sync up to your Dropbox account with a terabyte of data sitting in it. Do everything, many times, that might eat up memory or storage After all that abuse, see if the app holds up—most won't.

Squats Launch your app many times in a row. Repeat this until you have become mind-numbingly bored. Most apps will eventually crash. Many apps have intermittent crashes on launch as they use this time to initialize many things at once: network calls for the latest articles, or SDKs to ping with the users' location, or pulling in all the app state they saved from the last launch. Be aggressive and kill the app before it has had time to finish launching. Many of these operations are asynchronous and run in parallel, which is a recipe for intermittent crashes. Once you run into a crash, see if the user can recover by launching or reinstalling the app. If not, this is the deadliest of all bugs.

Prison Launch the app ignoring the different permissions that it asks for: deny it access to your contacts, or push notifications, or location data. Then you use the parts of the app that try to use this data. You will be surprised not just by broken functionality, but also by crashy behavior.

Cram build up lots of app 'state'. Add as many photos, emails, songs, drawings, etc., to the app as possible. It is far best if you can leverage real-world sets of documents versus taking the time to create either random documents, or manually create them. Real world data is full of awesome texture—make sure your testing uses as much real world test data as possible. A little known example that is amazingly useful, we used it at Google to test Exchange synchronization, is the Enron email corpus. Yes, thanks to the courts, a companies exchange server data was shared on the web; it is great real world data if you are testing a mail app. Similar test data corpora can be found for many data types—just look. Your app will eventually cry uncle and crash or freeze. It might take a a lot of data though...

Hidden Treasures explore seldom-used UI paths. Poke around in settings, or other hidden or least-used parts of the app. These areas are less tested and less used than others. They also often get less attention from developers or designers. Here lie many crashes. Arrrr.

Photo-bomb No, not picture taking. If your app is a camera app, run other camera apps in the background and switch between them. They are all competing for the same camera resource. Run many other large applications, or applications that run in the background just behind the app you are testing. Weird, mean, and ugly apps are best. Think of podcast and music apps, or Google+ or Dropbox with background image uploading and downloading. Especially think of apps that share the same type of background services that the app your testing uses. The more the likely to crash.

It Takes a Village Multiplayer games, especially ones with synchronized real-time player state (first person shooters, or racing games), often crash when connecting, or when different game states are reached or completed. Apps also get more crash prone when you have more players in the same game. Bring your friends, or a testing crowd to crash the party.

Dad's Credit Card Attempt to use content that is not yet unlocked or purchased inside the app, or only partially complete purchase and unlock attempts. Try restoring purchases many times. Not only are crashes frequent in these app flows, but also they can really make for cranky users because you are scaring them while their wallet is open.

Tips for App Developers

Red Pill Add a crash SDK to beta and production builds. There are many SDKs to choose from, and all work pretty well. These SDKs even prioritize the crashes based on frequency for you too. These SDKs hand you a stack trace and tell you what state the device was in when it crashed. Be brave and see your apps crashing. It is often far easier to fix crashes than you'd think.

Just Do It look at crash logs and fix them. This is likely the biggest developer issue with regard to crashes—they don't look at the crash logs! I've talked to many rich and experienced app development teams that say "yeah, we have crash logs, we try to fix a few every release". Fix them. Fix all of them. Fix them now. Fix them before any feature work. A new feature won't make users like you more if you are crashing. Do it for your career—if you point someone to the app you wrote, and it crashes, that's a poor resume.

Try and Catch me Add extra-defensive code around networking and dynamic layout code. If it can go wrong, it will. The network will fail you in the line of code right after the line that checks for connectivity. Layout change events happen while handling a previous layout change event. It happens. Exception handling and retries are your friends.

- **Never assume the network is available**--check for network availability, let the user know if it is missing so they can resolve it or forgive your app. The more networking errors you check for and catch the better off you'll be.
- **Actively monitor how much memory you are using** while your app is running. Monitor it both during

development, and while your app is running on the users' device. Heed the memory warnings form the OS and unload unneeded resources.

- XCode: Instruments can help here
- Android: DDMS is your friend.

- **Liberally log user actions and in-app events**, so when a crash does occur, you are more likely to know what happened leading up to the crash. Some crashes are difficult to reproduce, Logs can go a long way to help repro attempts.

Tips for App Product Managers

A Prioriti Make it obvious to your team the crashes are a top priority and to avoid them. The crash prevented is far more valuable than the crash caught in testing, and is more valuable than the crash found by an end user and fixed a week or more later. Reward and recognize developers and testers for finding these issues as early as possible. Crash prevention and resolution is an app feature, especially in mobile.

A Posteriori Make it obvious to your team that crashes in production must be fixed immediately. They should drop feature work to fix crashes. If you have a crash report, always deploy the fix—don't wait for it to be rolled up into a feature release.

Exemplar Apps

These apps represent the best apps based on this attribute. These apps just never go down. Try these apps out and see how stable they are and use them to inspire yourself that your app can be just as stable—it is possible to have a nearly crash-free app. Think about the great defensive code, the crash fixes, the reliable servers, the attention to detail, that these app teams must have.

IMDb Movies & TV
 Entertainment | Applause Score: 87/100

IMDb's Applause Stability Score: 78/100

Review, 5-Star, IMdb, iOS: "app works well; no issues. has all the features i need for quick questions and it doesn't crash with use." –wheatshock

Review, 5-Star, IMdb, iOS: "Better than the website for watching trailers n checking show times. Good stuff. Doesn't crash." – Olmansju

The IMDB app just never dies. This app leverages a lot of client server traffic, the team must have great error handling in the app's networking code.

Flashlight Ⓞ
 Utilities | Applause Score: 85/100

Flashlight's Applause Stability Score: 90/100

Review, 5-Star, Flashlight, iOS: "Doesn't crash! Unlike other flashlight apps" – DomDogg7

Review, 5-Star, Flashlight, iOS: "My toes thank you. Fast, doesn't crash, satisfying 'click' sound. Oh, and it does what it's supposed to do! Nice!" – IntuitiveUI

Yes, it is just a simple <u>flashlight</u> app. But, simple apps are less crashy.

Lets look at some crash-prone apps.

 Podcasts

Entertainment | Applause Score: 14/100

Podcasts Applause Stability Score: 9/100

Review, 1-Star, Apple Podcasts, iOS: "Crashes ever 30 seconds. New version crashes all the time (before a min). Plus the syncing is awful, it doesn't work it syncs all episodes downloaded or not." – Ben Yokitis

Review, 5-Star, Apple Podcasts, iOS: "crash crash crash. can't open the app. crashes every time. for weeks. even tried reinstalling. crap." – bronzini

Apple's podcasts app is perhaps the crashiest app built for iOS. The app makes many network connections, and pulls down quite a bit of data, but so do others that are far less crashy.

 Facebook

Social | Applause Score: 27/100

Applause Stability Score: 18/100

Review, 1-Star, Facebook, Android: "Crashes. Update borked everything. Bork Bork Bork." — Mike Haverty

Review, 2-Star, Facebook, Android: "Bugs. Crashes every time I click on an event. Hope you get this sorted soon." – Jolene McLaughlin

Review, 1-Star, Facebook, Android: "Getting from bad to worse! Keeps crashing! Every single time I want to invite a person to an event, the whole thing just crash! What is this weyh?! Keep asking us to update, taking up more and more space but the quality worsens! Fix it man!" – nicole chung

Review, 1-Star, Facebook, Android: "Junk. Facebook's app team can't write good code to save their lives. Constant crashes, constantly failing to post. They need to fire everyone on the dev team, scrap the current app completely and start fresh." – Doc Sprocket

Ouch. There are quite a few reviews that direct their crash frustration specifically at the development team. The Facebook Android app is by far the most crash prone of the major android apps.

Twitter
 Social Networking | Applause Score: 43

Applause Stability Score: 24/100

Review, 1-Star, Twitter, iOS: "Crashes like a demolition derby Read the title. Still can't help but crash." – The Yayo

Review, 1-Star, Twitter, iOS: "It crashes, it hangs. It crashes constantly. It hangs. You can't multitask, it forgets where you were. " – DMcMillan

It is surprising that the Twitter apps, both iOS and Android, are still so crashy this long after the acquisition of Crashlytics (a crash collection SDK), but it sure makes sense as to why they made the acquisition in the first place.

Tools and Services:

Crash Collection Every app should leverage a crash collection tool. These are little SDKs that you add to your application. They catch unhandled exceptions. They also capture a fair amount of device state, and capture log activity, so you can look for patterns in device state associated with impending crashes. These tools have versions for both preproduction testing and monitoring your real world users' crashes.

Crashlytics They are now part of Twitter. They do some deep exception catching work at the MACH level, and great reporting. The team in general is focused on the whole application lifecycle and have great, technical blog @ http://www.crashlytics.com/blog/

Crittercism A venture backed, fast moving service aiming at the full Application Performance Management space. It is a very solid exception and reporting service. Crittercism also has a blog that is worth checking out for some crash related trends:
https://www.crittercism.com/blog/

Applause SDK The Applause SDK is part of Applause.com (formerly named Apphance.com). The Applause SDK's key features are multi-platform support including Windows and the popular game development framework Unity. The Applause SDK also supports rich bug filing by beta testers. The bug filing supports screenshots and device state by default. Importantly, the Applause SDK supports an auto-injection service that adds the

SDK to your build without having to take code and integrate it into your code and builds. The Applause SDK is integrated with other crowd-sourced testing, app store review analytics, and automated test execution services, and powers some of IBM's Mobile First infrastructure. The Applause SDK also supports beta program management services. (Disclosure, yeah, I'm biased being the Director of Product for this and other services @Applause.com, but I, and the team, obviously care deeply about this space).

TestFlight/Others Crash collection is so important, that most app engagement, ad services, and beta management services (e.g. TestFlight, Flurry, etc.) are also adding crash collection to their SDKs as an additional feature. These crash collection solutions often aren't as rich in terms of reporting and less sophisticated in terms of crash collection, state collection, and are sometimes very 'chatty' on the network adding to app launch delays. You should avoid using these generic crash services and instead use dedicated crash collection services given its importance. TestFlight was recently acquired by Apple and has since dropped support for Android.

Review Analysis Use a review analysis tool like http://analytics.applause.com to search through app store reviews and find all crash reports from live users--they often tell you what was happening when the application crashed. Or, if you don't have that many reviews, just comb through your reviews manually and look for any mention of crashes.

Fragmentation Crash Automation It is embarrassingly easy to check whether your app has crashes on over 200+ devices via services like AppThwack. Their 'frictionless testing' services let you simply upload your build and it installs and launches your app on many devices. Their service then executes a few thousand gestures and reports any crashes. It is a great, quick way to cover Android fragmentation related crashes. Disclosure: when I started writing this, I'd only met the AppThwack team and been impressed with their automation—today my company has integrated their services into our platform—because I believed these guys built an awesome, low barrier and high value service.

Nerd Notes

You can extract the crash logs from devices. Here is a lot of information on how to get access to crash logs, and how to interpret them for iOS from Ray Wenderlich http://www.raywenderlich.com/23704/demystifying-ios-application-crash-logs. For Android: here is some info from uTest.com on extracting crash logs: http://forums.utest.com/viewtopic.php?f=17&t=2353

Quiz

Q: Any idea why Android users would complain a lot more about applications "hanging" than on iOS?

A: If applications are unresponsive on iOS, iOS will often just kill the app, where Android lets the application appear frozen and waits for the user to kill the application.

Quality Attribute: Elegance

"Is it the clumpy way he walks?
Or the grumpy way he talks?
Or the pear-shaped, square-shaped weirdness of his feet?
And though we know he washes well, he always ends up sorta smelly
but you'll never meet a fella who's as sensitive and sweet"

Fixer-Upper, Frozen, Disney

Attribute Definition

Users like pretty apps. When 5 different apps do the same basic task. They often pick the best looking one.

The development team of a very popular coffee app was busy focusing on the next version of its app, which would add new payment options, and take care of some critical bugs fixes. In the middle of a development sprint, their marketing director came running into the developer floor of the building asking what the heck happened to their app---it had dropped almost two star points over night. What happened? The iPhone5 happened. Users had loaded up the app on their new iPhone 5s, which were a few pixels taller than the iPhone4s.   Since Starbucks app (and most other apps) hadn't been updated yet, the apps were "letterboxed". Users went bananas.

Starbucks
 Food & Drink | Applause Score: 36

Review, 1-Star, Starbucks, iOS: "iPhone 5?????? Please make full screen compatible on iPhone 5'a beautiful retina display." -- Burbsman85

Review, 1-Star, Starbucks, iOS: "Needs support for iPhone 5. I love this app but the black edges on the phone at the top and bottom are very unappealing. Surprised it is taking so long for such a tiny change." --Rays

Users took to the app store to place reviews complaining about the clunky and outdated UI of this teams' app. Yeah, the team didn't have a bug, or server problems, or a new UX redesign that upset everyone, Apple simply updated the size of their phone overnight.

The development team was confused and said they were planning to update the look and feel in the next sprint. That wasn't soon enough for the marketing manager. Since the app reflected on the brand (2.0 stars next to your brand doesn't make a marketing exec very happy), the development team stopped their revenue-related update, made the app fit the extra 176 pixels, and immediately pushed an update. They won't take the elegance of their app lightly again. In fact, they completely redesigned and rebuilt their app recently to make the UI slick.

Elegance is about having an app that people find attractive. Not just useful and usable, but pretty. Apps have become accessories in our digital lives, and a clumpy, square-shaped app will cost downloads, user happiness, and reflect poorly on your brand. People are tired of the desktop apps, and form-based web apps and embrace the simplicity and elegance of modern mobile apps. The app stores highlight screenshots of your app before users decide to download it. If you are building an email client, they will look at other email clients and often pick the prettiest one. When your app is a bit clumpy, users will tire of it quickly—and post embarrassing reviews of how clumpy you look. In today's competitive app world, apps need to be dressed for success.

Elegance is very much about brands. If you are building an app and you either sell $10k watches, or you sell cosmetic products, you need an elegant app. A clunky app not only hurts the star ratings placed next to the brands logo on millions of devices, but it also undermines the brand outside of the app itself. Brands need to make sure their apps not only reflect their brand aesthetic, but also look great in the context of the mobile operating system.

Android. We talked a bit about the iPhone, what about Android? Every day, Android users are growing pickier about their apps' UI. Google has gone a long way to make sure their OS looks great. The first versions of android weren't so elegant. These days, Google uses words like "delight", "simplify", and "amazing" in their app design guidelines. If Google engineers are finally focused on elegance...you should be too. The Android team has created such a specialized design ethos around elegance, that if you make an app look "iOS7-ish", android users will again run to the reviews and complain. If your app is going to the opera--it should dress appropriately. If it is going to a Metallica concert-it should dress appropriately.

Flappy Bird is a notable exception to all of the above and all the below, but no one really understands flappy bird. We don't talk about flappy bird, as the app's success undermines the entire premise of this book.

Flappy Bird

Games | Applause Score: 67/100

Review, 5-Star, Flappy Bird, iOS: "The most terrible game ever. 5 Stars
I hate this game. But I play it. I don't know why. 5 of 5, would die again. And definitely will.UPDATE: I love that the FPS is improved. It helps. A lot. But I want the old graphics back. I feel like the retro look of the game gives it some class. I do not find the new pipe design appealing." -- Wade.Bieber

Review, 5-Star, Flappy Bird, iOS: "Dumbest game ever but so addicting!s
This game has awful graphics but you just have to bet your friends! " -- yrinirt

Technical Context

- **Difficult** it is difficult to design and implement an elegant UX. For many apps, it takes about as much time to technically design and implement elegance as it does to make sure the app functionally does what it is supposed to do. On iOS, many modern, fancy UX features like parallax, and dynamically generated blurry backgrounds, and animating things on and off screen where they start slowly and speed up are a few lines of code. On Android, it can mean using 3rd party libraries, or often resorting back to Newtonian mechanics and doing the math inside your app.

- **Tablet vs. Phone**: There is a big difference between what looks good on a tablet versus a phone. Especially for Android, the differences are major, as there are entirely different expectations of look and feel for tablets. Elegant tablet versions of many popular apps can look very different than their phone version—even having different use cases where the tablet version is for data entry and the phone for quick updates and read-only such as Microsoft's Android Office app.

Human Context

- **Many developers just aren't elegant** Look at them :) Developers, who are building the apps, usually think in terms of functionality by default. It is a rare bird that is both developer and stylish and thinks of elegance while they design and code. They need designers, or at best clone great design from other, similar apps. Rumor is that there are a few of these rare birds and they are often wearing skinny jeans.
- **Many apps just don't have designers** It is a fact that many apps don't have a dedicated designer, and understandably the design suffers.
- **Designers don't listen to users or industry trends** Sometimes designers just know their app is elegant, despite user feedback to the contrary. Sometimes they also just don't take the time to keep on top of trends or look at competitive apps. It is easier than most think. Just look to apps with great feedback on their UI, or pay attention to news events like apple's design awards and learn from the best: https://developer.apple.com/wwdc/events/awards/
- **App teams don't update often enough** some apps are marked "good enough" and left in the app store for months or years. Your app will get a weathered look if you aren't actively watching out for its UX. A great design is often the result of careful iteration. A great design can also go out of style.
- **No one on the team cares about design** Testing, Development, and Beta users, even management should all

a care about design but this is often not the case. Elegance impacts all disciplines and everyone on the app team speak up if they don't feel the app is pretty, or there are better looking competitors. Often, companies that treat their apps as just another client to their website aren't aware of design as something that requires careful attention in the app world.

Review Signals

If a review contains some or all of these words, it is often related to the Elegance quality attribute:

- alluring
- appealing
- attractive
- awful
- beautiful
- cute
- disgusting
- elegant
- gorgeous
- hideous
- inelegant
- stunning
- ugly
- unappealing
- unpleasant
- vile

App-Specific Sources

These are app-specific issues that strongly impact the elegance quality attribute:

- **OS UI** Users want an app that feels like an extension of their OS. Pay attention to how the OS does things, and really make sure you are smarter before you implement a custom button, a text box, or image picker. Custom UI controls are often a source of clunkiness. A favorite for customization is often the email and sharing options screens. Really make sure it is awesome, and works well, if you want to deviate from the standard OS UI.

- **OS Integration** Your app can show UX on the lock screen, on the home screen, in the sharing options, in the notifications window. Make sure your app looks great in these other contexts. If it looks out of place, your total app experience will feel awkward.
- **Screen size**   Common on android, many apps just look stretched out on larger devices. This is not elegant. If the app looks like a larger app, or web page, crammed into a small form factor, that's not elegant either. If the buttons are too big, or small, it can look dorky and be difficult to use. Design for the device sizes you are targeting.
- **On the go** Your app will be used in places you never expected. Is the app a very light color that gets washed out in bright sunlight? Does your app have cool stuff that flies in from the left on a swipe, but often triggers accidentally? Does your app have an awesome toolbar on top, but that is hard for users to click with their thumb while walking? Does you app have a drawer on the bottom, but swiping up often brings up the OS's control panel? Design for simplicity and clarity.
- **Competition** Most developers and designers think their app is pretty unique. It is not in the eyes of users. There are millions of apps. Millions. There are very likely 10, or 100, or even 1000 apps similar to yours. Why would someone download your app after checking out your screenshots? Why would a user stick with yours if another app, that looks prettier, is only a couple clicks away? Your apps should be elegant and standout in a lineup.

Example Reviews:

 Glympse - Share location with friends
 Navigation | Applause Score: 87

Review, 5-Star, Glympse, iOS: "I heart GLYMPSE

When I first got my first Glympse, I gasped, "OMG-this is TRULY USEFUL! I MUST HAVE this app!" Elegant in its simplicity, highly useful, easy to operate, you will wonder how you ever got along without it." -- Bill and Terry

Yahoo! Weather
Weather | Applause Score: 79/100

Review, 5-Star, Yahoo Weather, Android: "Best weather app on both android and ios
Clean, beautiful, and very informative. Other apps are cluttered and have less efficient UIs." -- Shannon Dobson

Tips for App Testers

The folks that test apps often find it difficult to test for elegance. Elegance is often viewed as an opinion, not a fact like a crash or broken functionality and testers consider themselves very rational beings. Testers often also validate against a spec—if the spec is a horrible design, they sometimes make sure that horrible design is implemented, and elegant deviations are all filed as bugs. In the modern app world, elegance is a quality attribute—it is as important, perhaps more important, than perfect functional correctness and reliability of the app. Great mobile testers will have a strong sense of design, know what the industry's best apps are doing with design, and file bugs and evangelize these issues with the rest of your team. A bad design is a huge risk for an app. Testers should pay attention. If something is ugly, or looks dorky, tell folks about it.

Top Elegance Test Cases

Hot or Not Compare the app you are testing with other top, elegant, apps. Look at how the sign in flow is done, look at how the settings are displayed. Consider whether you think people would say "pretty!" when they look at the app without even knowing what it does.

Fun town Don't just focus on functionality—ask if the app is compelling, engaging, fun, and even whimsical. When the app has errors, does it pop an annoying robotic dialog, or apologize profusely with a self-deprecating animation? Does the app look like very other app—if so, it is not likely to be viewed as stunning. Be careful though—animations or gratuitous fancifulness that gets in the way of the user getting things done quickly, or in the way of the content are a big "no no". Bug these to death! If you don't have a sense of humor, locate someone that does.

Thumbs Up can you app be operated using only your thumb? If someone needs to use two hands to use your app, you don't have an awesome design. Why do you think iPhones have remained small for so long? Even if the user is running a strange phablet or carrying their iPad on the subway, make sure most of the functionality is still accessible via the thumb and with one hand. The opposable thumb is what separates us from many other animals---lets leverage it.

Dolphins Evolve Opposable Thumbs

NEWS · Environment · Science & Technology · Science · Animals · **ISSUE 36·30** · Aug 30, 2000

HONOLULU–In an announcement with grave implications for the primacy of the species of man, marine biologists at the Hawaii Oceanographic Institute reported Monday that dolphins, or family Delphinidae, have evolved opposable thumbs on their pectoral fins.

Figure: Excerpt from theonion.com.

Pinch it Try many intuitive and interesting gestures and transitions. Does the app suddenly look awkward as it zooms in or out? Does the app respond quickly and in-sync with the gestures? Does the app make sure the gesture is discoverable to the user? Does the app hint that the UX is hidden off screen by bouncing the menu briefly into view? Does the app indicate, in a pleasing way that the gesture was processed by the app? Does the app support basic gestures that users expect? What about multi-touch? Pinch, pan, tap, swipe, rotate, and press and find out.

Table 1-1 Gesture recognizer classes of the UIKit framework

Gesture	UIKit class
Tapping (any number of taps)	UITapGestureRecognizer
Pinching in and out (for zooming a view)	UIPinchGestureRecognizer
Panning or dragging	UIPanGestureRecognizer
Swiping (in any direction)	UISwipeGestureRecognizer
Rotating (fingers moving in opposite directions)	UIRotationGestureRecognizer
Long press (also known as "touch and hold")	UILongPressGestureRecognizer

Figure: Apple's Documentation for Gesture Recognizers—try these on every screen.

Stretch-a-roo Try your app out on different-sized frames. These days, mobile devices scale from postage stamp size (Google glass and watches) all the way up to poster size (TVs). If your app is 'blown up' on a giant 8-in phone—you might look less than pretty. Make sure to evaluate all your app's resources to make sure they scale up to the very large and scale down to the very small. The Android development environment supports a lot of stretching and different resources for different device classes—but you need to test that your overall app experience scales up and down. Do menus or buttons look too tiny on a large tablet, or too small to click reliably on a mini-phone? Are the graphics fuzzy because they've been scaled up or down? Does the app's layout all get stuck in the upper left hand corner? Stretch it, squeeze it, try it on lots of devices.

Note: the Android emulator can be your friend. With the emulator you can create a wide variety of screen-sizes and DPI to checkout how your app's UI scales.

Tips for App Developers

Pre-fetch if you know you will need data, and what data you will need, fetch it before the user asks. Then you can look like a champ when you display it instantly, not just on-demand like an old school web link click. Pull all that data down locally and get it ready before the user asks for it. If you don't, your app won't feel buttery. Remember, today's smart phones are little super computers with lots of storage—leverage it for elegance.

Pre-Render How do those slick apps swipe and scroll instantaneously? They steal a technique from old computer game programmers—they render the next page before the users tries to view it. Use all those images and that text that you have pre-fetched from the server, and load it up in the UI elements, but keep them hidden off-screen until you need to page them in. This will make your app feel like it extends beyond the edge of the device, and the user will never have to wait.

Go Native It is very tempting to just load your responsive website into a hybrid app. This type of app can be built by a vendor in just days if the customer has an existing website. It is also tempting to just point users to a mobile web page. Your users will prefer the native version if you can afford to build a nice one. Native, especially on iOS, is just plain faster, looks better, and has lots of transitions and affects that you just can't get, at least not with great performance, with HTML5 today. If you want an elegant app, it has to be native.

Tips for App Product Managers

Read the news keep up to date with industry trends and information. Many apps were caught off-guard when iOS7 shipped with the new shiny look and feel—leaving most apps looking drab and out of place. Watch the latest app blogs, and you can even ask your developer to get the latest iOS or Android builds on your phone to experience how your app will feel on the next generation operating system. Most importantly—act quickly. Your users won't care that a new iOS7 build is coming soon after the day iOS7 comes out, or the latest Android KitKat OS with a lighter feel and wafers inside. Have your updated elegant app build ready when the OS is released. Oh, and ship your app the day the new OS comes out, not the day after.

Pixels Count Users expect pixel-level alignment. If your app looks sloppy, it will reflect on your service, brand, and it will bug them enough they might abandon your app. Designers should consider every pixel's role in your app. Negative space is great, if it should be there. Why is that button the size that it is? How far should that sliding menu come in from the left? Does that sliding menu overlap the edge of that profile photo and look awkward? Count your pixels before your users do.

Content is King On mobile, there's just not much room. Users don't use your app because your buttons and text boxes are awesome to look at. Design your app to maximize the room for content. Make content a top priority. Make it a top priority to keep your functional UX out of the way of the content. Use discoverable and intuitive gestures in place of UX widgets whenever possible. Only show widgets that are useful in the current context of the app. As with the design of the ironically named Chrome Web Browser—minimize your chrome.

Just Say No No Typing. Only do it as a last resort. Users don't like typing on mobile. At every opportunity, design your app to use canned options, default text, and auto-complete. Go to extremes to minimize typing in mobile apps. Desktop apps also have a lot to learn from mobile--just because you can type in text doesn't mean you should. Minimizing typing reduces user frustration, ambiguity, and speeds them to their goal whether it is cool news stories, calling a cab, sharing a web page, or sharing their high score. Just say no to typing.

Quick Read on Elegant Mobile UX via Gestures: a great, short, concise article (http://www.smashingmagazine.com/2013/05/24/gesture-driven-interface-2/) on gesture-driven-design by Thomas Joos.

Exemplar Apps

These apps represent the best and worst apps based on the elegance attribute. These apps are either just gorgeous or ugly ducklings. Look to these apps for inspiration in how to design your app. The list here is quite long as you have see elegance to, well see it. Take some inspiration from these apps.

Timely Alarm Clock
🎵 unknown | Applause Score: 76/100

Applause Elegance Score: 87/100

Review, 5-Star, Timely Alarm Clock, Android: "The most beautiful clock app on Android. And has a cool widget too!" -- Ruchir Sharma

Review, 5-Star, Timely Alarm Clock, Android: "The most beautiful android app I've used. Other UI designers should take lessons from this team. Not only does it have a super look and feel, it is the best time application I've used, with every basic watch-related feature you could want, from alarms, stopwatch with laps, countdown, and beautiful ringtone alarms too. Personally, I wish it had some productivity features to it, like task timing (using the timer to log time per task), and a calendar. But great job as is!" -- Jake R

Yahoo! Weather
Weather | Applause Score: 79/100

Applause Elegance Score: 87/100

Review, 5-Star, Yahoo! Weather, Android: "FANTASTIC! What else can I say. Same info as other apps, but this is app is GORGEOUS and the UI is intuitive."-- A. Scrubb

Review, 5-Star, Yahoo! Weather, Android: "Stunningly gorgeous app! The most beautifully laid out and practical weather app available. Tells me everything I need to know quickly, at a glance, in the most arresting format and background. Beats both Accutrack and my old favorite, AccuWeather, hands down! :-)Try it, you'll fall in love, because this app makes the weather look good on your phone even when it is a mess outside."-- Bruce Williams

Clear
 Productivity | Applause Score: 76

Applause Elegance Score: 97/100

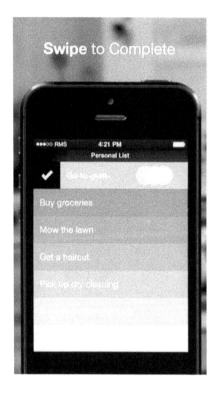

Review, 5-Star, Clear, iOS: "Very simple, very awesome! Clear is so simple, so elegant, and makes you focus on what really matters! Highly recommended!"-- Mohammed Bastaki

Review, 5-Star, Clear, iOS: "Amazing interface. Once you get used to it, it's incredibly intuitive. Very very cool. Simple and beautiful. Thank you!"-- Atanguay

Review, 1-Star, Clear, iOS: "Is that all you guy/s could come up with? Super Ugly Icon."-- Olatunji Babatunde

"You can please some of the people all of the time, you can please all of the people some of the time, but you can't please all of the people all of the time" – Abraham Lincoln

Cut the Rope: Experiments

Games | Applause Score: 92

Applause Elegance Score: 97/100

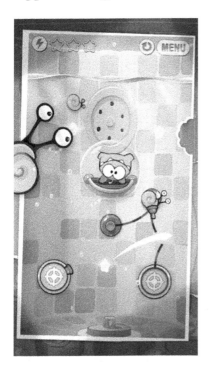

Review, 5-Star, Cut the Rope, iOS: "Very cute and fun I love the little creature. So cute."-- Cmfaythe

Review, 5-Star, Cut the Rope, iOS: "Beautiful Graphics and Game. Great game"-- Nwasgamer

Here are some less than elegant apps. You might call them monstrous.

 Yahoo! Fantasy Sports

Sports | Applause Score: 34/100

Applause Elegance Score: 6/100

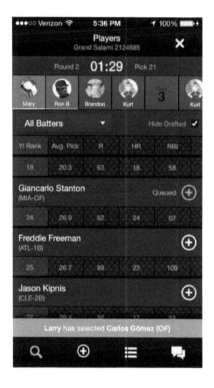

Review, 1-Star, Yahoo! Fantasy Sports, iOS: "HORRIBLE HARD TO USE. The design they have is so complicated and hard to use! They have everything black on black making this ugly and difficult. About to start a MLB.Com fantasy. Im done"-- mtz family

Review, 1-Star, Yahoo! Fantasy Sports, iOS: "Hideous. Difficult to read due to ugly monochrome background and small font. Would be nice to see head to head on same screen. Just a terrible app we are forced to use!"-- BirdsOnBat

Applause Elegance Score: 7/100

Review, 1-Star, ESPN SportsCenter, iOS: "First app was cool then they ' made it better' This app used to be fun and stylish now it is disgusting and slow"-- 1066080

Tools and Services:

UX Design Shops: If you don't know where to start, and don't have designers in-house, consider working with some experts that can work on your design or even build your app with a design-first approach such as Sourcebits.com. For European folks, Polidea.com is also another design and app vendor I can strongly recommend—their engineers are incredibly sharp and efficient. There is a long list of app vendors, too long and volatile to list them in a book. A quick Google query will get you many more folks willing to help you for a dime, but be sure to check out their portfolio of previously designed apps before giving them that dime.

Books: You obviously read books, so here are some great ways to read up on mobile UX/UI design:

- Android Design Patterns Interaction Design Solutions for Developers, by Greg Nudelman
- Mobile User Experience Patterns to Make Sense of it All, by
- UX Book Process and Guidelines for Ensuring a Quality User Experience, by Rex Hartson and Pardha Pyla

Get Quantitative and Data-Oriented: My team built the app store analytics at http://analytics.applause.com to support just this type of data mining. Applause Analytics has APIs that can show you the best scoring apps for any quality attribute in any app store and app store category. Data can be your UX friend.

Copy/Paste your best option is too look at great apps that are trying to do similar things. Let them inspire your design thinking. As you use mobile apps, keep an eye out for what works and what doesn't.

Quality Attribute: Performance

"To me, speed is really about convenience."
--Marissa Mayer

Attribute Definition:

Speed is king. Speed is a feature.

It is always your fault. Slow network? Slow device? Your servers slowed down? API calls? Is the camera slow? Your users only care that your app feels slower than they expected. They also have very little patience when they open your app for a quick second while they are waiting in line, and they get to the register before they can finish posting their latest selfie.

App speed is measured in milliseconds, not seconds. The average person starts to notice things aren't instantaneous after about 300ms. You need to be lightening fast or you will see reviews complaining about the performance of your app.

Many of the common performance issues in apps are either basic design issues, or the reliance on network services without caching. If your app is noticeably slow, and you can't get around it yet, some slight of hand can also help.

Review Signals

If a review contains some or all of these words, it is often related to the Performance quality attribute:

- cpu

- fast
- fps
- quick
- slow
- sluggish
- speed
- wait

Tips for App Testers

2400 Baud Users will be on slow network connections at the cafe, inside buildings, and on the edge of town. Test your app on slow networks. Do you get impatient with your app's load time? If you do, your users definitely will too. If you file bugs saying 'too slow on a slow network connection', it will often be ignored. Compare your app's load times, video load times, or recent news sync times with similar apps. If these other apps are faster on the same network connect speed, tell the team and point out the faster apps so they understand that faster is possible. There are always ways to make the app faster on slow network connections. You can quickly emulate slow network connections on android using the -netdelay and -netspeed flags on the emulator. On iOS, play with the awkwardly named Network Link Conditioner utility to simulate a variety of network speeds.

Impatience is a Virtue Be impatient when testing your app for functional bugs. Again, if it seems slow to you, users will think it is far too slow. The magic number is ~300ms. If any action in our app takes longer than that, users will notice. If actions are taking on the order of 1-2 seconds, you need to seriously revaluate how the app is designed and explore pre-rendering, pre-fetching, and the like described below. How to measure this response time? You can ask the developer to simply instrument the app with "timestamp breadcrumbs" before each click, and after the action is complete. Using your favorite mobile SDK and you can scan the log for timing info. Or, if can use an old-school stopwatch to measure load times, you know you aren't fast enough for discerning app users. Be impatient before your users feel the same

Load up that Server The app stores are great at app distribution, but not that nice about load on your servers. The day of launch can be a great one, or a sad one if you haven't tested your app's performance with your servers under load. Soasta.com among others like Applause.com can load your servers up to simulate launch traffic. If you have the time and technical chops, you can roll your own load tests using tools such as Apache JMeter or use a service like BlazeMeter.com. With your servers busy, try out your app's performance under load. If you don't plan for success, you probably wont find it.

Old School Users ask a lot of their mobile phones. They are downloading podcasts, uploading photo galleries, processing notifications, and apps are waking up with location updates. All

this can slow the device down. Too often, testing is performed on a device with nothing else running. Measure the app's performance with a busy device. Run your app on a lower end or older device. If you think about it, it is only logical that most devices in use are old, but testers usually focus on the latest and greatest devices. No one cares that your app is fast on the latest Galaxy, or 64bit iPhone. Make sure performance is adequate on older machines, or do the right thing and block install on these devices.

The Whole 9 Yards Performance is also about how long it takes a user to complete their task. Tasks can consist of multiple steps. Include the time it takes the user to find the next button. If the UI is confusing, or there are really fast-scrolling but long lists in the app, the app's overall experience can seem very slow. These days, users will blame your app if their Uber/taxi is slow to get there, or if they feel like it is a Sunday drive. Think about the performance of your end–to-end service. App quality doesn't stop with your app or server code.

Tips for App Developers

Cache Cache everything. Well, everything that's reasonable. Don't keep pulling your company's logo down via URL every time the app is launched. Unless you are building a real-time stock quote app, you can probably cache almost all your URL calls. It is too easy to do this right with libraries like <u>SDWebImage</u>. Cache. Cache. Cache.

Async The biggest performance issue that impacts users is a slow UX. A common cause is developers that perform computation or network calls synchronously, which makes the app slow or appear non-responsive to the user. Never run anything on the UX thread. If you are handling a button click, move the handler to an asynchronous message handler running on a different thread. If you want to do some state restoration or saving, don't execute it on the main/launcher code path. Never. The latest versions of Android actually try to prevent you from doing this at build time. Here is the basic <u>AsyncTask</u> pattern for Android development. On iOS it is up to you to know what you are doing. Use <u>dispatch_queues</u> and <u>sendAsynchronousRequest</u> networking calls. If you do anything on the UX thread, your users will notice.

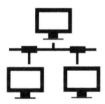

Network Profiling Often your app is slow because you are hitting the network. If your app includes other SDKs or social networking APIs, you may not even realize how network intensive your app has become.

A quick way to see what network calls your app is making, and how to slow they are, is to add the New Relic mobile SDK to your app. Use my referral code--if I had one. New Relic shows a very useful, and simple breakdown of everything slowing your app down.

Often apps try to pull a lot of state down from the server during the app's launch. Instead, defer every network call as long as you can. Run things in the background if you can. Don't slow down launch or user interactions with non-essential network activity.

If you profile your server, you can also track down what is causing the slowest of your network calls and fix the server latency in the interest of the app's performance. Server latency that used to be OK for desktop and web, will be likely be very poor on a mobile app on a poor network connection. Many top app teams also create dedicated APIs for their mobile app, even if they already have APIs defined for their web site. They often combine 3 or more chained calls into a single response as fewer network calls are generally nicer on the battery and speed up the app.

You will be surprised how much networking your app does, and how much it slows your app down.

Special note for mobile web and hybrid apps on iOS: A 300ms delay is built in. Crazy. It was added to Safari to enable the detection of double taps. Safari can't fire the click unless you know another one is coming or not--so it waits. There are a few ways to handle this: preventing zooming is one of them. Checkout a great article on this topic by Craig Buckler

Tips for App Product Managers

Misdirection When performance gets tough, the best app designers start distracting users. If you are waiting for 100 images to load you can avoid dreaded spinners, you can just show the images in sets of 5, and have some fun UX slide in as the next set of 5 finish downloading. Performance is half perception and half reality. Distracting the user with shiny things can go a long way to improving your app's perceived performance.

Kevin Leneway, co-founder and CTO of Haiku gave a great presentation on misdirection and other tips to keep your users happy and in love with your app. You can see the whole thing @ http://www.haikudeck.com/p/KvO0q6obER/haiku-deck-tips-and-tricks

Standards Set performance goals for your app. Make performance goals part of your app's core requirements, on par with the app's features. Measures often, and ideally measure every build in an agile environment, to catch performance regressions at the time they happen. Performance on mobile often requires UX and code design decisions—consider it up front.

Exemplar Apps

These apps represent the fastest, and the slowest of the bunch.

Applause Performance Score: 90/100

Review, 5-Star, Quip, iOS: "Super fast and easy! No nonsense app"-- Arsenal777

Review, 5-Star, Quip, iOS: "Fast, easy to use. Best mobile co-editing and sharing app.Freakin fast."-- Jacky Wang

Fandango Movies

Entertainment | Applause Score: 75/100

Applause Performance Score: 94/100

Review, 5-Star, Fandango, Android: "Fast and easy. Needed to buy my wife and the kids tickets for them and got everything done in 5 minutes. Sweeeeeeet."-- heythal1

Review, 5-Star, Fandango, Android: "Convenience through my thumbs. Fast and easy."— Steven Watkins

Infinity Blade

Games | Applause Score: 89/100

Applause Performance Score: 94/100

Review, 5-Star, Infinity Blade, iOS: "Good. Good game, with fast reaction time. Good fps. But shortish story."-- Slayerman28

Review, 5-Star, Infinity Blade, iOS: "Astonishing! This game blew me away with the graphics, FPS, and detail I would defiantly recommend this to anyone!!!"-- DatzwutSheSaid

The performance-impaired apps are below.

YouTube

Photo & Video | Applause Score: 20/100

Applause Performance Score: 19/100

Review, 1-Star, YouTube, iOS: "Terrible. This app is always freezing and slow... Rather use safari to get on..."-- ThisAustin

Review, 1-Star, YouTube, iOS: "Horrible fps. Every time I start watching a video, it goes to like 1 fps. I get stuck on one image for 1 second and it goes to the next image. Also, IT HAPPENS ON ADS!!! Fix this now."-- Airjaws

Facebook

Social | Applause Score: 27

Applause Performance Score: 33/100

Review, 1-Star, Facebook, Android: "Slowest app ever seen. This app... It is just so slow, I can't even use my device by Wi-Fi when it is on. Never seen this problem on other applications. But for example, when FB is on that's not possible to watch videos via YouTube mobile app because FB makes the Internet connection smoother. Just like a virus and unstoppable... I have 1gb ram dual core processor and android 4.0 and I didn't like this app at performance views."-- Eren Nacak

Review, 1-Star, Facebook, Android: "slow and poor performance. it takes around 50 MB of ram and is very slow"-- Usman Aslam

Tools and Services

New Relic for Mobile: Just drop their SDK into your app. New Relic then tells you everything about your http traffic latencies and importantly, if you run New Relic on your backend too, you can trace the entire end-to-end scenario to figure out what is slowing you down. Then you can see your mobile app's performance on the web, and of course via an their mobile app.

Crittercism: A leader in the crash and app performance space, Crittercism provides a broad spectrum of app monitoring features and is widely deployed. Very smart folks work there. Crittercism is an app SDK and provides web dashboards so you can analyze your app's performance. Alerts is a great feature to keep on top of your app's performance because none of us like staring at a chart all day waiting for it to change.

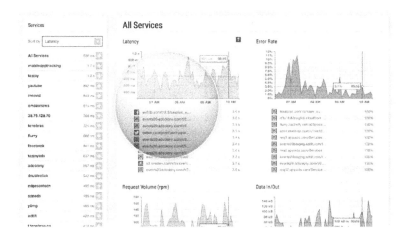

Quality Attribute: Interoperability

"Fools ignore complexity. Pragmatists suffer it. Some can avoid it. Geniuses remove it."
--Alan Perlis

Attribute Definition

The app world is getting more complex—both in hardware and software. I have an app on my phone to control the Phillips Hue lights in my office so it is that perfect dark blue that makes me feel like I'm writing underwater. I'm getting old and my right eye is a bit I have an iOS app that lets me control Google Glass from my phone. Jawbone speakers have an app for voice control. Pebble has an app that is an app store, to install other apps on your watch. How Meta is that? When I walk up to the headphones section in the Apple store, I get a notification about the products on display thanks to iBeacon. I use the iPhone's camera to scan the bar code of a Thunderbolt cable, and awkwardly put it in my pocket as I pass the security guard on the way out. The interoperability matrix for applications is only getting more complex every month. Will your app interact with hardware, Bluetooth, or soon drive your car for you? Users are starting to assume your app will act smartly with everything around it. They will expect your app to work with other apps and devices that you've never heard of, or that were created long after your app was deployed. Think about interoperability with apps, hardware, and other services before your users do.

Review Signals

If a review contains some or all of these words, it is often related to the Interoperability quality attribute:

- audio
- battery
- button
- camera
- compliant
- device
- export
- gps
- graphics
- hardware
- headphones
- import
- location
- notifications
- retina
- screen
- sound
- touch
- usb
- video
- wireless

Example Reviews

Philips Hue
Lifestyle | Applause Score: 31

Review, 1-Star, Philips Hue, iOS: "Can no longer connect to my bridge! 5s, Mini Retina, iPad 3, no dice on any device now..."--katsanes

Pebble
Lifestyle | Applause Score: 45

Review, 1-Star, Pebble, Android: "Works well previously. Used to love this watch before it was updated. It's buggy, connection is unstable and I have issues reconnecting each time it gets disconnected. Either it would render my blue tooth connection unusable and no matter what I do, it would not reconnect until I restart the phone. Please fix this asap, else it's just as bad as the Cookoo which I ditched for the pebble months ago!"-- Justin Gavin

MyGlass for iOS
Utilities | Applause Score: 60

Review, 1-Star, MyGlass, iOS: "Will not connect. I was so excited for this app but I can't get past the 'checking account' screen."-- Politicalduelist

Tester, Developer, and Product Manager Tips

Inter-App While you are myopically focused on making your own app awesome, users are bouncing between many other apps. If you are building a podcast app, switch between your running podcast app and a rival one. Make sure the audio transitions nicely, especially when connected to an external Bluetooth device. Copy/Paste different types of text between your app and other apps and validate that this is lossless. Seek out apps that use the same OS and device resources that your app does—and try to run them at the same time. If your app uses the camera, open another camera app in the background, open it to the picture taking screen and come back. If your app monitors the battery level, run it with other battery monitoring apps. If your Android app supports <u>Intents</u>, try to trigger those intents via other apps. Trigger intents when your app is running, and when it isn't running. If the app leverages social networking services like Facebook, try the app with Facebook installed and not logged in, installed and logged in, and not installed. Your app will behave very differently in these scenarios, and the app code has often has to handle different entry points to complete these different sign in flows. Where there is overlap or integration, there is often trouble.

System Interaction:
Consider integration with the OS. Here are several common areas of OS integration that are often the source of quality issues:

- **Notifications**: If your app generates local notifications, or accepts push notifications, be sure to check these flows with your app active with focus, active in the background, and not running. Try accepting notifications from the lock screen, versus unlocked, and while in another app. Many of these paths have very different UX and programmatic flows that you might not be handling at all, or poorly.
- **Bluetooth:** If your app leverages Bluetooth, test for all cases of disconnect, other devices, failure to connect, connections broken by system level toggles, and moving the device in and out of range. This is too large a test matrix to describe here, but read up on the platform's Bluetooth documentation, know all the states and flows, (documentation for Android, iOS). Consider all the possible failure modes, and test for them. Assume nothing will work right with Bluetooth until you have validated it. Test Bluetooth in real world conditions—in a variety of cars, different headsets, stores, and Learjets.
- **Permissions**: Your app has to ask for user permission to access many system services. Try your app in the mode where users declined certain permissions, and after accepting all permissions as a user can go into settings and flip these bits while the app is running. In these situations, the app should run with limited functionality, and

importantly prompt the user when they attempt an action that requires permissions the app is missing, and guide them through he process of fixing the permissions problem. Too often, users shut off permissions, and blame the app. It really is the app's fault if you don't handle these scenarios gracefully and handhold the user through the remedy.

- **Location Services**: Your app can look brilliant if you use location services correctly, and look like a buffoon if used incorrectly. If your app only needs city-level detail, make sure it doesn't ask for more. If your app only needs location info occasionally, make sure it doesn't ask the system constantly—it will burn up the battery. If your app doesn't register for location updates, it might get stale. If your app is only really useful while walking, use the location data to realize that the device is in a car moving 60mph and stop pushing notifications. Make sure your app checks the Accuracy of location info—sometimes it might be too fuzzy for your app to be useful, or it may look confused if it thinks you are across the street or on the other side of town. Getting location services into your app requires quite a bit of testing to make it great.

Candid Camera There are a wide variety of cameras on today's devices with varying speeds, options and image capture sizes. Many apps crash simply when they load unexpectedly large images. Some of these apps were developed years ago when 3MP was a good camera. Plan for the current and future crop of cameras.

Wired Plug your device into, and out of, everything. Try different headphones, speakers, different docking stations, car line-ins, etc. Look for any odd or out-of-order behavior

Exemplar Apps

Interoperability is hard. You can't imagine all the integrations and scenarios. You see this with the fact that the 'best' apps in interoperability have scores < 90. Interoperability is just difficult to get right given its complexity. These apps represent the best and worst of interoperating with hardware and other apps. Think about whether your app might have similar issues.

Applause Interoperability Score: 71/100

Review, 5-Star, Audible, iOS: "Simplicity and Integration. I love this app, especially now that I've discovered that it integrates with the Kindle app, and synchronizes across devices. So I can read on my iPad, listen along on my iPhone as I read on my iPad, or just listen. And the UI is simple and straight-forward, although I still haven't figured out how to purchase on the More Books screen - it's just kind of static and locked."— Darthenwald

These apps don't play nicely with others.

Applause Interoperability Score: 26/100

Review, 1-Star, Netflix, Android: "Fix Chromecast support. After update error keeps popping up saying device lost. Can't watch anything. (Nexus 5)"-- Vishnu Chandran

Review, 1-Star, Netflix, Android: "Mirroring sync issue with Samsung GS3 kitkat. Used to work fine before update to 4.4 but massive audio sync issue using mirroring over AllShare Cast Dongle. Not sure who's at fault, Netflix for not keeping up-to-date or Samsung for not paying attention to one of the most used apps on their devices"-- Chris Jones

Google Play services

Tools | Applause Score: 28/100

Review, 1-Star, Google Play Services, Android: "Rubbish. Dont see the point in it. It takes up to much room and drains your battery. But now i cant get onto youtube without it!"-- Emily Bunce

Quality Attribute: Content

"Who is rich? He that is content. Who is that? Nobody."
--Benjamin Franklin

Attribute Definition

For many apps, the content is the app. Content is king for news and social networking apps. The app is simply a vessel to deliver awesome content. If you area mobile developer building a shell for a website or service, your users will think your app is at fault—they don't blame the server or the article's author. As an app developer, even if you pull all your data from a server owned by another team or company, you can control a large part of the content experience by keeping the content fresh, making uploads and download fast, covering up mistakes or missing data pulled down from feeds. If you are a content-focused app, do everything to make the content the focus: put the content in a very nice frame, display it quickly, and provide for great transitions, content organization, and fix up as much of the broken content as you can locally. Even seemingly simple content apps have a lot of work to do.

Review Signals

If a review contains some or all of these words, it is often related to the Content quality attribute:

- accurate
- ads
- content
- correct
- data
- download

- information
- limited
- localization
- missing
- mistake
- precise
- sync
- translation
- upload

Example Reviews

Flipboard: Your Social News Magazine
 News | Applause Score: 84/100

Review, 3-Star, Flipboard, iOS: "Makes social enjoyable. Really really wish Pinterest feed was user's personal Pinterest account and not Pinterest Tweets. Who cares about their tweets when you can see this through Flipboard's twitter content? Please please work on this. I would use Flipboard daily instead of weekends only if Pinterest feed were an active part of it. Frustrating."-- BizOps

FOX News
 News | Applause Score: 45/100

Review, 5-Star, FOX News, iOS: "Michelle. Fox IS Fair & Balanced & I am so grateful to have a news source that I can rely on to give me both sides to every story! For every "debate" I find myself in, the facts from Fox News always has my back! Even if I can't convince myself correct, I give it some time for the event to play itself out, & I wind up w an apology every time....well almost every time, if the person is big enough to apologize, lol! Thank you again! Love & Peace to EVERYONE at Fox News."-- Michelle Ordway

Twitter

 Social Networking | Applause Score: 43 100

Review, 1-Star, Twitter, iOS: "Tweets not showing up. The app is great, but I'm having the same problem as a few other people have stated with their tweets & how they aren't appearing on the profile page. It'll show the last three tweets I posted from two days ago, until I click "view more tweets," then it'll show whatever was missing. The app is great, but it's just this bug that's giving me a hard time."-- ThatDoood

Tips for App Testers

AppBreeze Make sure the content is fresh, and in sync. This can be tough if the user is expecting the latest news or images as soon as they open the app. Monitoring scripts to check that the app is always showing the latest content is a great idea. Make sure the app automatically pulls down the latest content if left open for 15 minutes, or even a day. Test to make sure the app doesn't drain the battery too quickly in its zeal for pulling fresh content.

Retentive Mobile users can get persnickety when your app displays misspelled, or incorrect content. Even if this isn't your job, do what you can to make sure the folks producing and serving content that shows up in your app is correct. If an article contains a broken URL for an image, the app should detect that and display a default image. The app should also be resilient to articles with empty text and titles—it happens. Leverage proxy servers to intercept and force some of these error conditions and see how the app responds.

Tips for App Developers

No Moldy Bread If you wouldn't eat it, don't serve it. If you cache data or content, expire time-sensitive cached data. Respect the expire headers in HTTP requests. Tell the user if they are offline, and ask them to reconnect, instead of showing them articles from 5 days ago.

Trust but Verify Protect your app from bad data. When you get content from the server, check that it is valid. Content management systems (and the people who put the content into them) are notorious for having partial article information, broken links and broken image URLs. Sanity-check everything on the client side. When you detect bad data, decide whether to drop it altogether, or fill in with default values. Your app will look broken if things are missing, even if it was the server, author, or marketer's fault.

Pointcast Lives Think of all the ways you can pre-fetch or push the content to your app. Push notifications can be sent out to devices to tell your app to get the latest content. Push fresh content even when your app is in the background, or not yet launched. Make every effort to put the latest content in your app.

Tips for App Product Managers

Pull to Refresh We've all hit refresh on a web page to make sure we had the latest content—it is human to check, so make it easy. Make sure it is obvious to the user how to refresh their content and tell them if is still up to date. If you are an email or news app, even if you automatically refresh the content, make it obvious for the user how they can force a refresh, and to see that a refresh happened. Flipboard shows a spinner, and then flips the tile image on each tile independently. Flipboard also shows an alert at the top of the app when viewing articles so the user knows there is new content, and can click to have it refreshed without interrupting their current reading experience. Apple's mail client lets users pull down to refresh the content on demand. If your app doesn't support any of these, your users are trying to refresh and getting frustrated. Make refreshing of content obvious and intuitive.

I Want it All If your app only displays a subset of the content available on the related website—users will complain. A few years ago, it was OK to have a thin client. Today, users expect their apps to do everything. Many users around the world may only access your service via your app, so make sure it does most everything they need and not just a light version of your primary application. Users will also gladly compare your app with similar apps and want those other features whether you like it or not. If you leave something out, they will notice.

Exemplar Apps

These apps represent the best and worst of delivering awesome and interesting content to people.

Prismatic: Always Interesting

 News | Applause Score: 71/100

Applause Content Score: 87/100

Review, 5-Star, Prismatic, iOS: "My goto app and website for content. A fantastic app and website that does a remarkable job curating content. Recommended highly to news junkies that wanted to be amazed by everything they read." -- DBetebenner

Review, 5-Star, Prismatic, iOS: "Nice content and presentation. I especially like the way pages lock into place when flipping (snap to grid)." -- amcohen

Circa News

 News | Applause Score: 92

Applause Content Score: 87/100

Review, 5-Star, Circa, iOS: "Simplicity is Genious. Very simple and easy to use app, while still effectively communicating information. Highly recommend." -- Kayblayze

Review, 5-Star, Circa, iOS: "Meat without the potatoes. When you want to eat a steak you often get offered some side like potatoes. No one wants the potatoes. Circa gives the pertinent content without the unnecessary syntax. The follow option is great as well letting you follow as stories progress. This is news for the mobile world." -- Thromulator

Apps with questionable content attributes follow.

HBO GO
Entertainment | Applause Score: 33...

Applause Content Score: 39/100

Review, 1-Star, HBO GO, iOS: "Frustrated!!! App keeps freezing in the middle or end of videos! Constantly have to delete and re-install the app. One star for the content. It is all there but difficult to enjoy. Step it up, HBO!" -- Notttttt Impressed

Review, 1-Star, HBO GO, iOS: "So much publicity for a big fail. Dont ad stuff it does not work. Im suscribed via directv and hbogo says im out of region? Pleeease. What a waste of space in my cell phone. Do not download!!!" -- Johncoruna

Tools and Services

Proxy Servers Use proxy servers to inspect the content as it enters or leaves your app. Proxy servers also let you create custom, mock server responses to see how your app will behave with broken, empty, or malformed content.

Charles Web Debugging Proxy
www.xk72.com/charles | by Karl von Randow

Charles Proxy, and quick article describing how to use it with your iOS app.

Quality Attribute: Pricing

"The price of anything is the amount of life you exchange for it."
--Henry David Thoreau

Attribute Definition

App store pricing is a tricky thing. There is no one perfect price for everyone. There is no perfect mix of download vs. in-app purchases. Not even free is always a great price for consumers. People even complain about free apps—wishing they could pay to remove the ads. Even if they are OK with the idea of ads—if they get in the way of flinging a bird through the air, or they accidentally click the ads too often, they get upset. It would be interesting to see if the app stores would allow negative pricing, to pay users for app download, if only to see how people complain that they aren't paid enough. The bottom line is you will never make everyone happy with a perfect price for your app, but there are many ways to avoid the most common complaints about pricing.

Review Signals

If a review contains some or all of these words, it is often related to the Pricing quality attribute:

- affordable
- cheap
- cost
- exorbitant
- expensive
- inexpensive

- money
- overpriced
- pricey
- refund
- worth

Example Reviews

Microsoft Word for iPad

 Productivity | Applause Score: 35

Review, 1-Star, Microsoft Word, iOS: "Subscription fees for a word processor..? This is ridiculous, because I can pay 10 bucks for the apple word processor, and I can pay 10 bucks, one time. This isn't remotely worth it." -- Sorrien

Review, 1-Star, Microsoft Word, iOS: "$100 for a word processor that doesnt spellczhech???? The title says it all. this app is not worth the money if I have to transfer it to a computer to spell check and edit it. there is no excuse!" -- Chernandezthegreat

OmniGraffle

 Business | Applause Score: 58

Review, 5-Star, OmniGraffle, iOS: "Buy it. Amazing. A little pricey but provides a lot of bang for the buck. App would be perfect around $29.99." -- SayNo2Ads

Review, 5-Star, OmniGraffle, iOS: "Apple-class. Very impressed with the quality of OmniGraffle: it feels as powerful as any of Apple's iWork suite (and as well designed). I initially held off because of the high price, but now I think it's worth every cent." -- Steve T-S

Candy Crush Saga ®

 Games | Applause Score: 65

Review, 1-Star, Candy Crush Saga, iOS: "Money wasting. I got the app candy crush and it was very fun in the beginning. I loved the strategy but then you needed to buy power ups and they cost me so much money! I spent over $30 for nothing! I suggest you honestly not to buy this" -- Poopy123456789

Review, 5-Star, Candy Crush Saga, iOS: "NEED MORE LEVELS!!! MORE LEVELS!! Been waiting over a month now. The second world add on was great, but still not enough. Come on now. Anyone complaining about not being able to beat a level or spend money should shut it. I haven't spent a dime on lives or bonuses. And if you don't have friends who want to help you cross a bridge just unlink your Facebook account and do the 3 levels to unlock it. BOOM!" -- David Dickerson

Tips for App Testers

Be Transactional A sure-fire way to upset users when it comes to money is to fail in the middle of a transaction. If users are trying to make an in-app purchase, and they aren't sure if it was successful, this can cause a lot of angst. Test the app flows around in-app purchases very carefully. Turn off the network, close the app and restart it while trying to make a purchase—make sure the app recovers nicely and messages the user nicely about both failed and successful transactions in all cases. After purchasing something in the app, make sure that is visually obvious to the user.

Billboards Ads aren't a necessary evil—especially if they are large or in the way. If you are accidentally clicking ads while testing the app, your users will too. Try using the app one-handed, or on a bus. If the ads are just way too distracting, it is a quality issue. Push back on design to make sure that accidental ad clicks can be avoided.

Restoration It happens. People upgrade their devices, have multiple devices, and restore their device state, or delete and re-add your app to the same device. Make sure the purchases in all these scenarios are restored, or you are sure to bring on the ire of users. They will hunt you down in app store ratings and social media for 99 cents.

Tips for App Developers

Careful with Money Your code that deals with purchased items is hallowed ground. Carefully consider all failure scenarios. If there is a way a purchase can fail, it will. Read the platform-specific documentation for in-app purchases thoroughly, and handle all failure and retry conditions. Apple documentation (https://developer.apple.com/in-app-purchase/) and Google Play Documentation (http://developer.android.com/google/play/billing/billing_overview.htmldocumentation is extensive, but you are well advised to sit back with a coffee or two and read.

Don't Roll Your Own If you can avoid it, leverage 3rd party services and APIs that have covered all the corner cases for you already. Rolling your own is a bad idea. Look to third party services like Parse.com, Stripe.com, or UrbanAirship.com to do your heavy lifting.

Tips for App Product Managers

Sticker Shock Compare your app's pricing with similar apps. If your app is charging more than competitive apps, users may have too high an expectation of quality or feature set in your app, or complain about your app when they find a less expensive alternative. Pricing is a quality, and perception issue, not just a revenue issue. Don't charge a crazy amount for your app just because you can or it will hurt your star ratings and overall sales.

Exemplar Apps

Plants vs. Zombies
 Games | Applause Score: 94/100

Applause Pricing Score: 96/100

Review, 5-Star, Plants vs. Zombies, iOS: "Fantastic and cheap! So much entertainment value in this purchase. I have an extreme dislike for IAP, but it seems that the amount of coins that are needed to buy game modes is obtainable by playing through the whole adventure mode. I'm appalled by the "pay a little, get a little" system that are in so many games now. I prefer games to be an all-you-can-eat buffet." -- Зяболка

Review, 5-Star, Plants vs. Zombies, iOS: "Worth Every PennyKeep it up!" -- Hhhhhhhifsnf

Here is an App that is not such a good deal. Surprisingly it is almost the same game—just version 2 of the awesomely priced app above. EA bought PvZ and they apparently intended to monetize the sequel. Interestingly PvZ 2 has 20X fewer reviews than the original PvZ.

Plants vs. Zombies™ 2
 Games | Applause Score: 51/100

Applause Pricing Score: 33/100

Review, 1-Star, Plants vs. Zombies 2, iOS: "Ripoff. Future world gets stupid hard. Was able to beat all other worlds without using power ups but past level 9 it gets ridiculous. Obvious cash grab and explains why pop cap fired 20% of their workers: they weren't making enough money so let's make it harder. Now buying gems for the zen garden? Total scam tons of obvious paid 5 stars to go along" – Easy evue

Review, 2-Star, Plants vs. Zombies 2, iOS: "Ruined with micro-transactions. They made the game much harder to try and make you spend real money to beat it. But it's not even that that ruins it, it just feels like the micro-transactions are over done, that all there is to do in this game, at every opportunity they ask you to spend real money. Very disappointed with the second installment of an amazing game" – HashtagAtlanta

Tools and Services

Parse.com (http://www.parse.com): Now owned by Facebook, Parse simplifies app development through their services. Parse supports simple, and secure in-app purchase support among many other commonly used services.

UrbanAirship.com (http://www.urbanairship.com): An early pioneer in making all app features easy via their web services, check out Urban Airship's in-app purchase support.

Stripe.com (http://www.stripe.com): Stripe accepts payment without going through the app stores, allowing you to bypass the app store fees. Stripe also has some local UX libraries and

functions to make accepting payments a breeze.

AppAnnie.com (http://www.appannie.com): App Annie provides for deep tracking of your download and in-app-purchase revenue, as well as some awesome competitive analysis—see how other apps are monetizing and moving up or down the app store rankings.

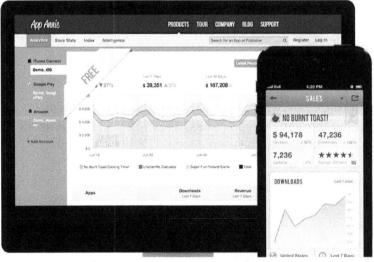

Quality Attribute: Privacy

"Privacy is not something that I'm merely entitled to, it's an absolute prerequisite."
--Marlon Brando

Attribute Definition

Privacy is a hot topic among apps. The more you ask about the user, the more paranoid and skeptical they become. The more you know about the user, their location, friends, messages, the more convenient and smarter your app appears. This is a classic space-time tradeoff between utility and exposure. Like security, privacy is often a matter of perception. Make sure your users believe they are getting a fair exchange of value in return for giving up some of their data.

Review Signals

If a review contains some or all of these words, it is often related to the Privacy quality attribute:

- anonymous
- confidential
- fraud
- identity
- information
- personal
- privacy
- private
- scam
- spam
- steal

- trustworthy

Example Reviews

Chrome Browser - Google
Communication | Applause Score: 51/100

Review, 1-Star, Chrome Browser, Android: "Canceling Google. Google wants total control of every thing I do. I wish I never got Google. It could be great if you didn't 't have to give up your privacy as they can tape whenever they want, you in your daily life. They can also take pictures, so cover your camera holes. READ the terms or you will give away your rights." – Karen Skinner

Review, 5-Star, Chrome Browser, Android: "Almost perfect. Be careful with your privacy and this browser" – Omar Sueque

Angry Birds
Games | Applause Score: 85/100

Review, 1-Star, Angry Birds, iOS: "Bad. Letting the NSA spy on people is terrible! Shame on you! I want my money back!" – John1981ads

Jelly
Social Networking | Applause Score: 48/100

Review, 1-Star, Jelly, iOS: "Read the TOS before you create an account. Per the Terms of Service, you can remove the app from your phone, but Jelly won't remove you from the service. They haven't responded to support queries about whether or not your identity will still be used once you've removed the app." -- SFheather

Secret - Speak Freely

Social Networking | Applause Score: 68

Review, 4-Star, Secret, iOS: "Chaos. When I first discovered this app, I thought it would be mutual ground for fun, friendship, and learning. It very quickly took a bad turn at my school. Kids have used it to make fun of the most innocent people and ruin them. This needs to be completely anonymous, no connection to contacts. I'm just lucky I've been sparred so long. " -- TheMoosner

Review, 1-Star, Secret, iOS: "Anonymous? Let me get this straight: I downloaded your app to check this anonymous social network and the first things you ask me is:1) My email address2) My phone number Maybe next time. " -- madsenlima

Tips for App Testers

Data Hoover Think about the data your app vacuums up: social network profiles, friends, pictures, text messages. Understand every point in the app where it asks for permissions to access the user's social networks, location, device and data, and make sure your app needs the data. Make sure the app uses the data. If your app doesn't use the data, it shouldn't collect it in the first place. Testers should question whether the user knows why the app is asking for the data access, and how the app will use that data. Data access should be minimal and obvious or your app's perceived privacy will suffer.

Data Spillage Question how the app treats user data—does it post contacts or other data up to their server without telling the user? Does the app over-share location or email addresses on social posts? Does the app write private messages or photos to the local file system where other apps could access it? Enter private data into the app, use it, and look for any of this data showing up in the clear on the network or local storage. Test that all appropriate private data is removed when the app is deleted from the device. Even Snapchat didn't actually delete the photos in their first app version.

Tips for App Developers

Careful What You Ask For Only access data, or request permissions for data you need, not just data you would like to have. The less data you access, the better for your app. Only access location information as infrequently as you need it, and with as little detail as possible. If you do an OAUTH request to a web service, only ask for the pieces of data you actually need. If you allow authentication via Facebook, don't ask for info on the user's favorite books just because you can.

Follow the Data Be super careful where you store your data. Parts of the file system can be accessed by other apps, and sometimes over a USB tether if the phone has debugging enabled. Don't store any data longer than you need it. Don't put data anywhere if you don't remove it during uninstall. If you no longer need a particular permission, remove it from the manifest. If you are passing personally identifiable information to a 3rd party log function, or a 3rd party SDK is collecting information—you are responsible for what happens with that data after it leaves your app. Either block the 3rd party code from getting that data, or verify that it is securely handled. Follow that sensitive data from cradle to grave.

Tips for App Product Managers

Puppet Master Privacy is half perception. When you get access to user data, make sure the user feels they are very much in control of all actions taken with their data. If the user ever feels they've lost control of their data or social network activity, they will complain just before they delete your app, and it will reflect poorly on your brand. Small things like having a button to trigger spammy social posts, rather than automatically triggering the social dialog, goes a long way. Product managers shouldn't be puppet masters, Pinocchio didn't like it much.

Ask When an app asks for permission to access private data, first explain to the user why you need the data, and what you will do with it, before the system asks. On iOS, users are prompted for permissions inside the app when your app asks for it, so be sure to have plenty of in-app explanations of why you need access to private data or services. Pop a dialog just before the system surprises the user with a warning. On Google Play, be sure to have clear permission reasoning in your app description on Google Play as the users is asked for permissions before downloading the app. Brenden Mulligan posted a great write up (https://medium.com/on-startups/96fa4eb54f2con) how to design for permissions with details, and some analytics on user engagement with different app flows and designs.

Plausible Deniability If you don't ask for it, you might not blamed if private data leaks via another app. When a user's selfie is leaked on their social network and you haven't asked for camera roll permissions, or social network access, you can claim innocence even if yours was the last app they remember using. Your app can be suspect even if you didn't leak private data.

Exemplar Apps

Evernote
 Productivity | Applause Score: 74

Applause Privacy Score: 89/100

Review, 5-Star, Evernote, iOS: "Best Productivity App. I love this App! I use it for business and for saving all my personal information, especially great memories with the family! This app has 'saved' me many times!!!!!" – RDL Co

Review, 4-Star, Evernote, iOS: "Need Privacy Improvement. Great app! Definitely one of the better ones on the market. However, it could use an option to opt-out automatic sign in, or implement a passcode feature, every time you start the app. You know, so you can keep your private entries private." – LA3211

Path
 Social Networking | Applause Score: 85

Applause Privacy Score: 83/100

Review, 1-Star, Path, iOS: "Over 700 One-Star Reviews. Path users have never quite gotten over the fact that their personal contact information, (all their friends, family and associates details), were put on Path's servers without their knowledge. So where is the giant description that reassures those people who abandoned Path that it is safe to come back in the water? Writing good code is important. But making users feel like you're not stealing their private info is equally important. Path has a long way to go before it can woo back those lost customers. 'One bitten, Twice shy.'" -- Pro App Reviews

Review, 5-Star, Path, iOS: "Simple and privacy. I love path it more privacy and what i love the most it really a path that actually can says where u have been to" -- Mama Qilah

Angry Birds
 Games | Applause Score: 85

Applause Privacy Score: 83/100

Review, 1-Star, Angry Birds, iOS: "NSA. Is this the angry birds that downloaded all my information and gave it to the Government?" – Hdjdjdjsopl

Tools and Services

TRUSTe: Consider the privacy standards, and testing, provided by TRUSTe. They have a great list of things to look for specifically in mobile apps, and they can help you with privacy issues and perception.

Appthority.com (full description in security section below)

Quality Attribute: Security

"We will bankrupt ourselves in the vain search for absolute security."
--Dwight D. Eisenhower

Attribute Definition

Security is a large topic. Security is everything from user names and passwords, data protection, malware, and hacking. Security is about the reality and the perception of these things. Your data needs to be secure, act secure, and look secure. There is always a tradeoff between usability and locking down your data and services—users will complain about both no matter what you decide. An app has to let people in before it can secure their data.

Review Signals

If a review contains some or all of these words, it is often related to the Security quality attribute:

- account
- captcha
- encrypted
- hack
- sign in
- malware
- password
- safe
- secure
- security
- spyware
- steal

- stolen
- unencrypted
- virus
- vulnerable

Example Reviews

HBO GO

 Entertainment | Applause Score: 33

Review, 2-Star, HBO GO, iOS: "It was excellent... Until the problems started. It worked great for a week or so, and one day it wouldn't let me sign into my account. Then it started saying things like 'An Internet Connection is needed to access the HBO Go app. Please try again.' I have perfect Wi-Fi connection . I've tried deleting the app, but nothing has worked. Please fix this someone! I just want to enjoy myself some Game of Thrones marathons" – Sabine Strasburger

Review, 2-Star, HBO GO, iOS: "Forgets sign in information. Every couple of days I have to reenter my AT&T sign in information, and that makes this app painful to use." – pederb72

Snapchat

 Photo & Video | Applause Score: 45

Review, 2-Star, Snapchat, iOS: "Big hack problem. So I got a snap from my friend but it's said I already opened it but I didn't and it wouldn't let me replay it and to day I got another snap from a different friend on a different day and it said I already opened it but I didn't and I can't replay it on a different day and I know you get a replay once day and I haven't used the replay both days and it says they sent three snaps to my friends and she got no snaps from me. This is a really big problem" – Gabby19231

Note: it is all perception at the end of the day

Review, 1-Star, Snapchat, iOS: "Too many security holes. With the recent breech of cell phone numbers tied to accounts, and recent reports that ddos attacks launched against the app can cause the phone to crash. The app has a nice concept, maybe when the developers address such MAJOR issues; then I'll re-download it." – deepdivermw

WeChat
Social Networking | Applause Score: 61

Review, 1-Star, WeChat, iOS: "Worse and worse. No security, always feel like someone is monitoring , no privacy, reliability . Whatsapp is way more secure than this . Don't waste your time" – aragon731

Review, 1-Star, WeChat, iOS: "Chinese scam. Awful app... They gather info to spy on us. Impossible to delete the account or delete the profile pic. SCAM be careful" – Loudj

Tips for App Testers

Account Testing:

- Try to sign in when there is no network, or weak network connections. Does the app display helpful messaging or just fail silently?
- Test the username and password variations allowed by the backing web service. Too often, the app won't pass special characters, or has different case sensitivity, so users can't

sign in with their existing account. This is a major issue across all apps.

- Forgot username or password flow? If your app doesn't have this functionality, you need it, or many users can't get into your app.
- Can the user delete their account? Does deleting their account remove all traces? Test for this.

Tips for App Developers

Basic Securi-TEE Too many apps don't do the basics. All HTTP network connections should use SSL/HTTPS. Encrypt, obfuscate and hash your data with a bit of salt--all of it. Especially data that gets passed to 3rd party software and SDKs. There's no reason these days to ever store your app's data in the clear. Don't give Forbes a chance to write about your app's security issues, perceived or real: (http://www.forbes.com/sites/parmyolson/2014/01/16/starbucks-chose-convenience-over-security-in-leaving-ios-app-vulnerable/)

1/16/2014 @ 5:16PM   10,556 views

Starbucks 'Chose Convenience Over Security' In Leaving iOS App Vulnerable

+ Comment Now   + Follow Comments

Is it better for mobile apps to be easy-to-use, or secure? It's a question that app developers constantly grapple with in the face of a competitive landscape, and it can sometimes take a data breach like Snapchat's to push them in the latter direction. Earlier this week security researcher Daniel Wood disclosed his findings on how Starbucks SBUX -2.11% was storing data about users of its iOS app in plain text and locally on a device, making passwords and even geolocation data about users vulnerable to theft if the wrong kind of hacker got hold of their iPhone.

Starbucks has said it knows about the app's vulnerability and that the possibility of it being exploited is "very far fetched." It says that none of the app's 10 million users have come forward to claim their data has been misused as a result.

(Photo credit: @staikadam)

Sign in Caution Use extreme caution when signing users in, or creating accounts. Keep checking to see if the network connection is valid. If there is any issue during sign in or account creation, do all you can to functionally recover and display hints to the user on how to resolve the problem.

Tips for App Product Managers

Making Appearances You can have the most secure app in the world, but be sure to let your users know. If they don't know it is secure, they often assume otherwise. Explain to the user how much you value their trust and the lengths the app goes to secure their data. Tell them what you don't do with their data. When you make security improvements, tell the world.

Vigilance Pay attention to the news and blogs with regard to app security. If someone else has a security issue, users will ask the same of your app. Path was found to be grabbing user's contact lists locally and pushing that list to their servers. Nothing nefarious, but bloggers got hold of that revelation and within 24 hours the other apps were franticly removing the same innocent functionality before they were singled out too. Be proactive and fix issues reported in other apps before it is found in yours. You might not even change your code, but the perception of your app's security can change overnight.

Let Them In A key source of app frustration is creating accounts and signing in. Typing in a mobile app is painful and error prone—avoid it if you can. If your app doesn't have any need for locking it down, don't ask them to create an account, and delay signing in via their social network it is needed for the app's functionality. You will lose countless users at the door. Smashing magazine has a great article on simplifying account creation and sign in in general.

Exemplar Apps

Applause Security Score: 67/100

Review, 4-Star, eBay, iOS: "More secure. This is a great App but it needs to be more secure. Not 100% safe. Don't leave your account on. If you are done ALL WAYS LOG OUT." – More secure

Applause Security Score: 20/100

Review, 1-Star, Starbucks, iOS: "Frustrating app. I regret downloading this new version. It keeps logging me out and refuses to recognize my password. Very frustrating!" – Ponderhim

Review, 1-Star, Starbucks, iOS: "Spilled milk. Oh StarBUCKs, ye have faltered. Such fine beverages but such poor IT testing. The new app is spoiled milk in our expensive cappuccino's. Password rarely works and the actual gold card (yes the one u make us crave) fails to load. So I have a prepaid card I'd live to whip out and use on my phohne, yet is a flop..." – Yokaze

Here is a quick interview with Alex Waldmann, a mobile app security consultant in the uTest community.

Q: Hi Alex, you are a security expert in the uTest.com community. How many apps have you seen during your security work?

A: I've faced more than 250 different applications, from a variety of verticals and applications types including B2B and B2C applications on web, mobile and desktop. The apps we analyze cover a wide range of different businesses. These include audiobook online shops, eBook readers, auction houses and social market places, document management platforms, survey apps, payment processors, global brand websites as well as medical document cloud solutions, premium content subscription newsstands, corporate websites, intranets and many more. It is satisfying to see that companies from all kinds of businesses have started to understand the importance of regular security audits from experts outside their own ranks. But I personally think that the percentage of companies caring about their user privacy is still too low in an IT landscape that is highly connected and exposing lots of entry points to attackers.

Each of these projects was a unique challenge and required a deep understanding of the customer's business to be able to carry out a proper vulnerability assessment not only covering purely technical flaws, but also identifying issues in the business logic that only human security experts can identify.

Q: What can you say about the state of app security today? What is the level of maturity compared to desktop?

A: Most web applications still use highly vulnerable technology stacks, mostly because there is a low entry barrier for developers and the famous security by obscurity pattern is still widespread. Developers rush to implement new features and impress their managers and customers, while proactive application security integration into the SDLC, automatic scanning and manual penetration tests from outside experts are shoved into a backlog of important things. They usually end up neglected until the first major PR disaster because of a security breach.

I see a trend in applications either having a very high level of security or being extremely poorly designed, on a 50/50 distribution. Secure apps use up-to-date, robust frameworks and libraries and apply best practices in development, so there are usually only a few minor slips in attention of the developer that cause minor vulnerabilities that are quickly discovered. The other half of poorly designed apps generally tend to have vulnerabilities from all of the OWASP Top 10 vulnerability categories and never cease to amaze our team of security experts. It is incredible how insecure applications can be, given the vast amount of best practices documentations on platforms such as http://owasp.org/ that should be a standard resource for any developer that is into web development or has to create an HTTP/HTTPS accessible API.

Q: Do you have a formalized set of tests that you run on all apps? Or is security testing on mobile very specific to each app?

A: One of the unique aspects of our offering is that we have standardized our testing practices as much as possible, but also incorporate a custom risk assessment and an individual test plan, catering to the needs of the customers' business and the application type. Web app security is not adequate for mobile app protection requirements, which is why we at uTest have built a set of specific attack scenarios for our experts to carry out against mobile applications. We use different test cases, some containing over 100 different high-level attack scenarios. This gives our international tester team the inspiration to find new attack vectors specifically tailored to different application types such as Digital Rights Management or flaws in payment systems.

We strive to constantly improve our process, streamlining the testing and reporting workflow while also extending our list of known flaws based on what we've seen in-the-wild. We have a large database of attack patterns and flaws that have been proven to be critical to our customers' business. This allows us to quickly cut through the noise from the output of automatic scanners and programmatic audits, getting straight to the critical vulnerabilities.

Our testing is follows standardized testing methodologies, industry best practices and we focus on the OWASP TOP 10 (https://www.owasp.org/index.php/Top_10_2013-Top_10s) vulnerabilities. The OWASP Top 10 vulnerabilities are based on datasets from firms that specialize in application security, including consulting companies and SaaS vendors. Their data spans over 500,000 vulnerabilities across hundreds of organizations and thousands of applications. The Top 10 items are selected and prioritized according to this prevalence data, in combination with consensus estimates of exploitability, detectability, and impact estimates and allow us to accurately rate the security threat level for target applications and to focus primarily on issues critical to the core of a business.

One example of our specialization is our own unique testing methodologies for businesses that deal with the protection of digital goods, assessing the security level of Digital Rights Management (DRM) apps on web, mobile and desktop.

Q: What are the most common vulnerabilities you have seen?

A: In our testing we often identify systemic vulnerabilities like Cross Site Scripting (XSS) or a complete lack of protection against Cross Site Request Forgery (CSRF), possibly because it is hard for a non-technical manager to grasp the impact of these types of vulnerabilities. If the developers are not used to protecting their apps against these attacks, and they don't believe in the impact these can have, it can be hard for them to justify the additional time that is required to properly secure their applications.

We are limiting the number of individual reports for issues that occur in every component of a system to a minimum. They wouldn't provide much value to the customer and are actually dangerous because they might tempt developers to check-list fix only the individual occurrences of an issue that were reported instead of addressing them through a change in the technical base of the application.

The highest numbers of individual reports for vulnerabilities we get are for Cross Site Scripting (XSS) and Authentication/Authorization related flaws. Looking at issues that we find in almost all applications, missing security related HTTP headers, insecure cookies and information disclosures are very common.

Q: What is the most misunderstood thing about mobile security? Any myths?

A: "If they can't see it they can't hack it."

On a mobile application, not just the interaction with the interface and the code on the device can expose vulnerabilities, but also the backend which is usually the entry point for an attacker. Even with the rise in processing power and memory size, most mobile applications are still powered by a server backend, typically consisting of servers exposing an API (often RESTful) with communication over HTTP. If you want to evaluate the level of security of your application, make sure you understand that your backend and its APIs will be easily exposed to anyone with sufficient technical knowledge and it will be subject to attacks. Just because you can't see it when interacting with the app doesn't mean it is safe from manipulation. Security testing your mobile application should focus on testing the security of your backend as that is the usual entry point for attackers - your servers are likely holding all the valuable data.

Q: What was the most dangerous or interesting security issue you have found in mobile apps?

A: It's hard to choose from the variety of critical flaws that were identified.

Here are my top 3 critical vulnerabilities:

Top 1 - Intellectual benefits: We gained access to a library of thousands of professional audiobooks by simply changing a download link ID. This allowed an attacker to download all eBooks free of charge with a single purchase of any one eBook from the library.

Top 2 - On a dating web application, it was possible to see any users plain text password by simply adding them as a favorite and looking at the HTTP request sent to the backend. This also allowed reading out the mobile phone number and email address of any user without purchasing a premium service package.

Top 3 - The ultimate goal for many security researchers is the classic remote code execution flaw (RCE) which is the worst possible vulnerability type in regards to its exploitability. This flaw allows hijacking of the entire server and possibly compromising the entire network and mobile app client. We have found dozens of variants of remote code execution flaws and subsequently discovered many more flaws in the target system by accessing the source code of the application on the server by exploiting this vulnerability.

Q: Generally do you think native, hybrid or mobile web have the most security vulnerabilities?

A: Cross Site Scripting on mobile devices is lately evolving into a serious issue and this isn't about popping a funny alert box on the device screen. Using WebViews in hybrid apps can expose your users to all kinds of mayhem if an attacker can inject JavaScript into the web content requested within the WebView. The JavaScript is often able to access an exposed API of the application itself and can subsequently carry out actions on behalf of the user within their session. A common location of this weakness is a forgotten password web form embedded via WebView into an app.

Forcing SSL/TLS (including proper certificate checks & hostname checks) on any communication between the mobile device and your backend is a must. Developers should also make sure they understand who they are exposing APIs to and what access is really needed. An excellent resource on WebView security aspects is the publication "Attacks on WebView in the Android System" at http://www.cis.syr.edu/~wedu/Research/paper/webview_ac sac2011.pdf

As most of the vulnerabilities are discovered in the backend (API) of the application, it pretty much does not matter if it's a native, hybrid or mobile web app.

Q: What is it about mobile app security that is so interesting to you personally?

A: As a security researcher, it is frustrating to see that so many companies are still neglecting security and their users privacy, exposing sensitive data or documents. Mobile application security right now is like web application security during the early days when you could simply Google millions of platforms that are vulnerable to SQL Injection and everything you touched during an audit broke apart quickly.

Enterprises and startups alike need to start embracing a proactive approach to application security. This includes inviting external experts to help look at the applications and the business behind those applications to get a new perspectives of what types of attacks are likely.

During our risk assessments, customers are often shocked at what types of attacks they or their developers never thought of, mainly because they don't tend to think about how to attack applications 24/7.

So for me personally, what's really intriguing is that the amount of issues and the criticality of the issues that are widespread among mobile applications with a web based backend, are at an all-time high. This is both satisfying for a tester as well as frightening.

Q: If you look forward to 2017, what do you expect to be different in the mobile security world? Please give us a glimpse into the future.

A: I expect a 50/50 distribution for mobile application security, similar to what we are seeing right now on web applications, highly secure or really weak. Frameworks for mobile applications are maturing and the importance of user privacy and the integrity of the backend behind it are more widely accepted. There are numerous courses to take as a mobile app developer and so apps will be either seriously tightened up by developers that embrace security as a core principle in development or the apps are very insecure when the developers neglected any security aspects completely.

Here are the top mobile-specific security suggestions from Alex Waldmann:

Security by Obscurity - Why obfuscation matters

100% security is rarely achievable, and nearly impossible on complex applications. Your goal should be to raise the bar for attackers so it's no longer cost-effective for them to attack your application and making it much more difficult for them to get anything out of your application.

Obfuscating your applications code is an important step to protect your applications integrity, especially if you are required to hard-code crypt keys into your application. With Android applications it is trivial to decompile the app file (APK) and view the source code and extract secrets out of it.

Don't trust your clients: App security vs. backend security

Even with the rise in processing power and memory size, most mobile applications are still powered by a server backend, typically consisting of servers exposing an API (often RESTful) with communication over HTTP. If you want to evaluate the level of security of your application, make sure you understand that your backend and its APIs will be easily exposed to anyone with sufficient technical knowledge and it will be subject to attacks. Just because you can't see it when interacting with the app doesn't mean it is safe from manipulation. Security testing your mobile application should focus on testing the security of your backend as that is the usual entry point for attackers - your servers are likely holding all the valuable data.

Watch out for Cross Site Scripting

Cross Site Scripting on mobile devices is lately evolving into a serious issue and this isn't about popping a funny alert box on the device screen. Using WebViews can expose your users to all kinds of mayhem if an attacker can inject JavaScript into the web content requested within the WebView. The JavaScript is often able to access an exposed API of the application itself and can subsequently carry out actions on behalf of the user within their session.

A common location of this weakness: forgotten password web forms embedded via WebViews into your app

Mitigation: Force SSL/TLS (include proper certificate checks & hostname checks) on any communication between the mobile device and your backend. Make sure you understand who you are exposing APIs to and what access is really needed.

Protect your data at all times

Whether in transit or at rest, your users data should be secured against access from outsiders, for example against malicious 3rd party applications on the same device or attackers on the same insecure network (imagine a public Wi-Fi) sniffing the communication between the device and its backend.

Using SSL/TLS is important but not enough. If you want to take it to another security level, use best-practices for REST API authentication http://www.thebuzzmedia.com/designing-a-secure-rest-api-without-oauth-authentication/ and hash and sign your requests to protect them against tampering.

Tools and Services

Learn what apps do

Appthority.com provides a comprehensive set of analytics and tools to automatically assess the security of any app. Appthority performs static, dynamic and behavioral analysis. They can disassemble your code and look for vulnerabilities, look for any data leaks while the app is in use, and scan for any sketchy app behaviors that are specific to certain times, places, or events. Use this tool to understand the security of your app, and any other app in the app store.

Quality Attribute: Satisfaction

"There are some days when I think I'm going to die from an overdose of satisfaction."
--Salvador Dali

Attribute Definition

Does your app satisfy your users? That's the end game. There are different apps for different folks. Some folks want to be distracted while waiting at a bus stop, some challenged by a puzzle, and some directed around town. Apps satisfy these users in millions of ways. Some satisfy better than others, and those apps appear to be winning. Apps delight with engaging and beautiful UX, connecting them to new friends, making their email feel less like work, making their selfies look awesome, and bonding with offline brands and experiences. At the end of the day, apps need to satisfy their users or they won't share it with their friends, and will stop using the app. Satisfy your users. If possible, make them love your app and brand.

Review Signals

If a review contains some or all of these words, it is often related to the satisfaction quality attribute:

- addicting
- addictive
- boring
- charming
- crap
- delightful
- disappointed

- engaging
- enjoy
- favorite
- fun
- recommend
- regret
- waste
- worthless

Example Reviews

Review, 5-Star, Threes!, iOS: "Addictive and beautiful. I love this game! Very addictive and satisfying. The faces on the tiles give the game a fun character." --Oldbay777

Review, 1-Star, Tinder, iOS: "What's the point of this? I can't message or match up to any girls on the app. I feel like it is a waste of time. I mean, out of 1,473 girls... Not one was a match? Ok... Lame app" -- Saint Tokyo

Review, 5-Star, Tinder, iOS: "Simple easy entertainment. Fun app, definitley entertaining. Have not had sex with anyone I met on the app which is a downside" --Polaske

Review, 5-Star, Mailbox, iOS: "Email is fun again. Love the design and feel when I use it. I wish I could make it my default mail app. Can I?" -- olucho

Tips for App Testers

Sad Pandas Listen to your dissatisfied users. It can be tough, but you need to listen. Find their issues in the app store reviews, via your in-app feedback tool, or on social media. Fix these things, by documenting and tracking them. Share this user pain with the developers and product owners to make sure they know what their audience is thinking. Always be driving fixes in your app to make these sad pandas less sad. You can't make everyone happy all the time, but it is your job to try. What tester can turn down free bugs?

No Backlog of Sadness Most things that make users sad have made them sad for a long time. They might tolerate your app for a while, but eventually give up on you if you aren't fixing these nagging issues over time. Don't let your team ignore these issues sprint after sprint. Highlight these sad or frustrated users during stand ups. Advocate for these folks and get these bugs fixed before features happen.

Tips for App Developers

Avoid the Couch Avoid the team having a formal intervention with you. If your testers or product owners are passionate about what seems a trivial bug, or a minor UI change, don't ignore them if they show you how it might impact user happiness. It is easy to get caught up in the feature backlog, even crashes, but ultimately the app's goal is to create passionate and satisfied users. Listen to feedback, give a little, and avoid the couch.

Tips for App Product Managers

Happy Snowmen Seek out compliments. Find out what makes your current users happy. Find out what makes them share your app with friends. Find out why they love similar apps—maybe your app can be similar. Find these happy snowmen in app store reviews, in-app feedback, and social media. Share their happiness with your team to remind them of the awesome impact they have on real people in the world. Ignore any fake reviews you submitted yourself. Just imagine how much cooler your app will be…in summer

Clown Around Delight your users. Don't just accomplish the task. Your app should have a personality and do at least a couple

amazing things; a surprisingly dramatic or amazing UI transition, anticipating the users next step, turn something difficult a single click, have some whimsical text tucked away somewhere. Even Apple's Siri is a little playful. Focus on surprising your users with great functionality, speed, and a little bit of fun.

Exemplar Apps

TripIt - Travel Organizer

Travel | Applause Score: 76/100

Applause Satisfaction Score: 76/100

Review, 5-Star, TripIT, iOS: "Get This App! Saw TripIt advertised on a Virgin America inflight commercial and gave it a shot. Planned a 2 week, whirlwind trip through Australia and New Zealand with multiple flights, hotels, ferries, trains and it automatically created an accurate, concise itinerary by scanning my email. I loved it! Kept the trip organized and accessible with just my phone. Also easy to share your plans with friends and family who want to keep track of your plans. Would recommend to anyone." -- TiogaGrandma

Review, 5-Star, TripIT, iOS: "Love tripit. One of my favorite and most recommended apps. Creates a useful travel log of all my journeys."—RTFSTF

Now an app with not-so-satisfied users.

AIM (Free): Free SMS, Chat, Group Chat

Social Networking | Applause Score: 32/100

Applause Satisfaction Score: 21/100

Review, 1-Star, AIM, iOS: "Disappointed. This app has so many bugs: delayed sent/received messages, completely missed messages, etc. Some stupid arguments/disagreements could have been totally avoided if these bugs didn't happen. Do something about this AIM!!"— Skins-Fan

Review, 1-Star, AIM, iOS: "PHAIL! I've had this app for a while and ever since the last update, it's been crashing and not letting me send ims to offline users :/ and wtf is lifestream? Take that crap out! I already have a Twitter ;) but srsly, I'm pissed that I updated my aim to have it being messed up now. Fix it asap. K, thanks! "— L.

Tools and Services:

Apptentive.com (http://www.apptentive.com) profiled in detail earlier, Apptentive provides a two-way feedback channel with your users, inside your app.

Quality Attribute: Usability

"It is far better to adapt the technology to the user than to force the user to adapt to the technology."
--Larry Marine

Attribute Definition

Usability means building the app for your user, not building it for you. Don't get between your user and what they are trying to do. Your app should be intuitive, accessible, and obvious. Your app should get out of the way. Other than when you are doing some super cool transition in the UX, the user should often forget that your app is there, and be focusing on the content or the experience or the service. Usability is perhaps the toughest quality attribute to get right.

Review Signals

If a review contains some or all of these words, it s often related to the usability quality attribute:

- accessible
- blind
- bugs
- control
- deaf
- difficult
- disabled
- easy
- frustrating
- gameplay

- interface
- intuitive
- layout
- restrictions
- simple
- useful
- ux

Example Reviews

Clear
Productivity | Applause Score: 76/100

Review, 3-Star, Clear, iOS: "I want to be able to move items. Such a pretty app. Such amazing tactile feedback, especially with the sound effects. I feel like I've accomplished something momentous when I swipe. For these reasons, I continue to use it. But please, allow me to move items between lists. Try this: go download Readability, see what happens when you swipe to delete an item in that app...whoaaa! A list of options? Delete, archive, star, etc? Copy that functionality exactly, except add a "move to another list" option. Don't spend 8 months doing it, either. This should be easy, and all these reviewers on here shouldn't have to tell you how to do your job."— Gehrkenstein

Gmail
Communication | Applause Score: 45/100

Review, 1-Star, Gmail, Android: "Gmail user interface is very damn nice but the attachments downloading and sending can't function properly. Couldn't download. Touch to retry. Was what I always get when I try 'viewing' or 'saving' an attachment. Pls fix. I need it for school use very urgently! "—Gabriel IsGabriel

Spotify
Music | Applause Score: 76/100

Review, 4-Star, Spotify, iOS: "Time will tell if UI worth it. I have an iPhone 5 with iOS 7.1 and for me this last update was a major performance hit. The new interface is beautiful but songs are lagging and it seems to have issues loading (caching) album artwork. The other feature I miss is being able to tap on the song playing and from there go to artist or album. The new UI makes scrolling required on smaller devices. If this theme could be skinned to have performance and beauty I'd give 5 stars. Still my top streaming app and a wonderful product guys ! "— rockchalkjhawks

Tips for App Testers

Be the User While testing for functionality, think about the usability too. Try testing using only one hand, with only your thumb. Are all the controls reachable? Are the most common actions the easiest and most obvious to accomplish? Test the app while on the bus, at the park. Ask random people if they can quickly accomplish quick tasks on your app. If you have to ask or think how to accomplish something in the app it is a bug.

Accessibility Your app will be used by all types of people: Old, young, deaf, blind, color-blind, far-sighted and people from very different cultural contexts. Accessibility is a topic that warrants its own book, but here are some platform-specific pointers that will ramp you on the basics for apps:

- **Android**: Android publishes <u>accessibility testing checklists</u> (<u>http://developer.android.com/tools/testing/testing_accessibility.html</u>). Test to ensure your app is usable via the D-Pad (directional pad) on Android SDK versions 15 and below, and Gesture Navigation on higher versions. Also, try driving every feature of your app via TalkBack and Explore-By-Touch—if you can't, it is a bug.
- **iOS**: Apple shares an <u>accessibility testing guide.</u> (<u>https://developer.apple.com/library/ios/technotes/TestingAccessibilityOfiOSApps/TestAccessibilityonYourDevicewithVoiceOver/TestAccessibilityonYourDevicewithVoiceOver.html</u>). Enable Apple's Voice Over mode in the system settings, and drive your app. To really make sure folks that can't see well are able to use your app, use the Device Screen feature to literally turn off the display during your testing. Test that your app is usable in high contrast mode. Check for any UI that becomes hidden or merged together. Here is a sample of the many accessibility options available on iOS, test your app with these options enabled:

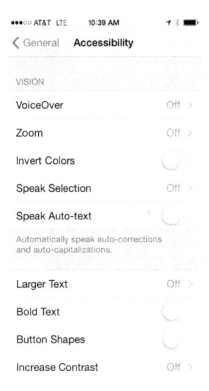

⟨ General   **Accessibility**

VISION

VoiceOver   Off ›

Zoom   Off ›

Invert Colors

Speak Selection   Off ›

Speak Auto-text

Automatically speak auto-corrections
and auto-capitalizations.

Larger Text   Off ›

Bold Text

Button Shapes

Increase Contrast   Off ›

Consider these while testing each accessibility setting:

- **Voice Over** Explore your app making sure that each
  control has accessible labels and accessibility Hints and
  Traits. If you close your eyes and Voice Over isn't
  descriptive enough to figure out how to use your app—it is
  a bug. Note, you can also use the Accessibility Inspector
  with the iOS Simulator to view the accessibility properties
  of all UI elements.
- **Invert Colors** Check that buttons and text and UX element
  boundaries are generally still clearly visible.
- **Larger Text** Enable this, and go back to your app to see
  that Text isn't wrapping incorrectly, or missing because it
  doesn't wrap at all. Make sure your app actually displays
  larger text—sadly, many apps don't respond to this
  accessibility option.
- **Button Shapes** With this option on, make sure your
  buttons look reasonable—it adds a border to all buttons, but

custom-drawn buttons could look aesthetically awful, unreadable, or confusing with this option turned on.

- **Audio** Change the audio properties and check any audio playback in your app. For example, you might discover that your app is only pushing out audio to the left ear.

Tips for App Developers

Respect Authority Users expect to control their accessibility settings across all apps—but that can only happen if you respect the authority of these global settings. On iOS, support dynamic text by using UIFont and preferredFontForTextStyle: methods. On Android, when specifying font sizes, use Scale Pixels, and your app will respect the users large font accessibility settings. Be sure to leave enough room to show text with these larger fonts.

Labels are a Good Thing It is easy, but many developers just don't know about this, or know how to do add them to their code. On iOS, add labels, hints, and sometimes Traits to all your interface elements so the system can read them out loud to users who can see. On Android, add android:contentDescription to any UI control that could use some explaining, and be sure to add android:nextFocus properties to every control to make sure the D-Pad, gesture navigation, and TalkBack will list controls in the right order. Also check for Accessibility events, and trigger them when things like notifications or brief messages appear. Labeling is easy, and it is the right thing to do.

Stock Unless it is a marquee feature of your app, don't write custom controls. The stock UI controls exist and have been tested time and again by the community—you'll never have the time or knowledge to make your customer controls perfect with respect to rendering or accessibility. Be very cautious in building custom controls. The more custom, the more dangerous it is with respect to overall usability and app quality.

Tips for App Product Managers

Keep It Simple Stupid The simpler you keep your UX and UI, the fewer usability or accessibility issues your users will find. This is also the least expensive way and fastest way to build apps. When in doubt, use the defaults and most common practices and common designs for functionality—they are that way for a reason. Both iOS and Android have reams of UX guidelines to read and follow. The more buttons, textboxes, gestures, the more complex your app gets, the more likely something happens that you didn't expect, and the more planning, designing, testing and user education you will have to deal with. The more custom your app is, the more expensive, less agile, and more testing it requires. Be smart, and keep it simple. This KISS principal is the single most valuable piece of advice for app PMs—it impacts every quality attribute.

Accessible Design Design for accessibility. Make Accessibility part of your specifications. Make it part of your design. Make sure your app responds to, and enables, the OS's accessibility features. If you are a large company, there may be legal or business/market ramifications for not supporting Accessibility in your apps. Focus on Accessibility because it is the right thing to do.

- **Android**: Android has a rich set of accessibility features (http://developer.android.com/guide/topics/ui/accessibility/index.html,
- **iOS**: Apple also has a long list of accessibility features (https://www.apple.com/accessibility/ios/), and also shares an accessibility testing guide. (https://developer.apple.com/library/ios/technotes/TestingAccessibilityOfiOSApps/TestAccessibilityonYourDevicewithVoiceOver/TestAccessibilityonYourDevicewithVoiceOver.html)

Data Talks Instrument your app with engagement metrics. There are many services to choose from, but the key is to ensure you are looking at the data. Look for user activity that is more popular than you expected. Optimize the app's UX design for frequent use scenarios aiming for fewer taps. Naïve user click/engagement folks always think more is better—it is often just poor usability or relevance. If the metrics on these frequent use cases aren't quite what you expected, consider changing your app's focus and purpose. Look for scenarios that users just aren't engaging—consider making them more discoverable, or removing them altogether. Look for gestures, where your app doesn't respond—these are hints that your app isn't behaving like the user expected. (AppSee.com automatically discovers these no-response gestures for you). See where in your app the users are hanging out most, and where they aren't, and adjust your app design and product planning "lean startup" style.

Exemplar Apps

Walmart
Shopping | Applause Score: 69/100

Applause Usability Score: 91/100

Review, 5-Star, Walmart, Android: "Right at home. Easy. Convenient. Used this application to order birthday gifts for my daughter. Love it. Plus easier to browse here before I go to the store in the crowd" -- MsBrwnNProud

Review, 5-Star, Walmart, Android: "Intuitive interface and easy to use. Simple and user friendly " -- Giriraj VG

Inside.com has mixed usability reviews, showing that there is a lot of variance and opinion from users in the usability area.

Inside.com - Breaking News
News | Applause Score: 63/100

Applause Usability Score: 56/100

Review, 2-Star, Inside.com, Android: "Don't like UI or understand why random stuff is in my feed. You can swipe to see more in topic, but also if you scroll up you end up seeing the same content again. Also, seeing topics that I haven't favorited...don't even know where my favorited topics are showing. It is more like "their feed" than "my feed." " -- Roquentin72

Review, 4-Star, Inside.com, Android: "Just 1 suggestion. I love this app, it pulls very interesting/funny stories and makes it easy to share them on Facebook/Twitter. The one suggestion I'd like to make to developers is the ability to save a story, so I can go back and read the full article later. If this feature is already available, it is not easy to locate. Thanks for the great app!" -- Dusdkod

Review, 1-Star, Inside.com, Android: "Bad usability. Doesn't really work as promised. You can choose topics that interest you, but the app ignores your preferences and shows you whatever. My hunt for a useful news app for my phone continues. " -- fenix692

Netflix

Entertainment | Applause Score: 31/100

Applause Usability Score: 36/100

Review, 1-Star, Netflix, iOS: "Subtitles are painfully small. The new update made the subtitles extremely difficult to read. They are 1/18th and inch tall on my iPhone. Not comfortable at all!! " -- Blwillia

Tools and Services

UserTesting.com is a fast-growing service that gets your app in front of real mobile users, and records their reactions and thinking as they attempt to use your app. It sounds like a great idea, and is a little fun, but it can be time consuming to watch the videos versus a more formal usability report, from a real usability engineer. The users aren't always your target audience either, but when there is a mismatch the videos can be entertaining to watch. The basic price is right and you can get feedback very quickly (less than an hour) using this mobile-focused user testing service. If you are building an enterprise app, it is very likely worth the time and money to investigate their enterprise offerings which give you access to a usability expert to organize the testing and give you a summary of the findings.

XCode's Interface Builder lets you quickly add labels, hints, and traits to every control.

iOS Simulator lets you quickly load your app up and visually verify that all controls have accessibility markup for labels, hints and traits. It even lets you add them quickly and test them out before adding this data via interface builder or Objective-C control creation code.

Section III: App Store Analytics

There are hidden treasures and lessons to be gleaned by looking at all reviews, reviews per app store, and reviews per category. Below we explore some of this interesting data to discover what quality issues you should focus on even if you haven't started building your app, or have an app with no reviews at all. We explore the data in search of evidence that Agile and Lean engineering (shipping frequently), leads to better quality. Here are some early findings from analytics on over 200 million app store reviews, across millions of apps.

Distribution of Quality Scores

The distribution of app quality scores across the entire store is interesting. The two points to note here are that the spike at 100, is primarily due to small apps with very few, but all 5 star reviews. The other peaks are also due to apps with smaller numbers of reviews, but consistently got reviews with the exact same star rating, which maps to perfect 1,2,3,4 or 5 stars on this chart. There is definitely a bias toward positivity in the app reviews.

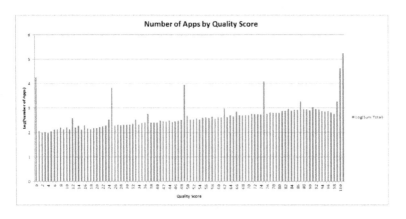

Cross-Store and Cross-Category Star Ratings

Looking at the average star ratings per-app-category, and per app-store, there are a few major observations to be made. The app stores are very similar in terms of user happiness with their apps when comparing the across similar categories of apps. The ratings difference between the platforms is only about a max of half a star rating when compared category to category. This is pretty interesting as it suggests parity between the platforms in terms of how much users are claim to like their apps. Where one store is better than the other it seems to be an even split as well—it is not as if iOS or Android dominates across all categories. iOS users are happier with their games, medical and business apps. Android users are happier with their tools, navigation and weather apps. These differences are only slight but also agree with what you might generally expect given the strengths of the underlying platforms.

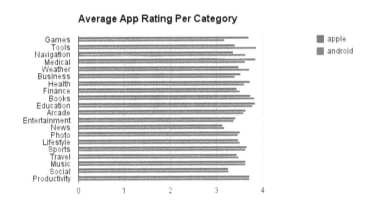

Average App Rating Per Category

Cross-Store Category Attributes

The types of review chatter vary widely across app store categories. Within each app store category, users are talking about some topics more than others. You should find your app's category in Appendix A, and use it to guide your development, testing and product management quality priorities. Focus your quality efforts on the areas where there are more reviews—those are the areas where users are looking most. Also focus extra effort on the areas where apps in your category do very well—this is where the competition is.

The frequencies of attributed reviews can vary widely across categories. In the games category, the most common reviews are talking about satisfaction and content. While in the finance category, the chatter is all about security and usability. If you are building a game, focus on the game content and making users thrilled and excited. In contrast, if you are building a finance app, it is most important to focus on the usability and security aspects of your application.

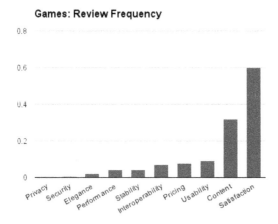

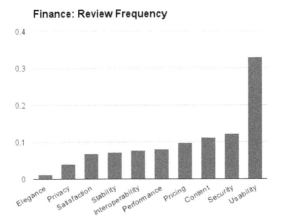

Finance: Review Frequency

Focusing on the average review scores in each category can give you insight into which attributes are the easiest and the most difficult to get right. This view can also clue you into what makes users in these categories happy. In games, privacy and stability are the most difficult quality attributes to get right, so focus on those early to stand out from your competitors. When building a finance app, it is ironically difficult to get a lot of positive feedback around pricing, easier to get usability right, and far more difficult in general to get all those Scrooge McDucks out there to be satisfied with your app.

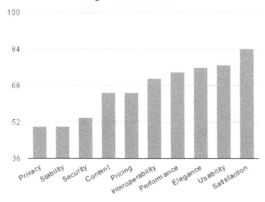

Games: Average Review Score

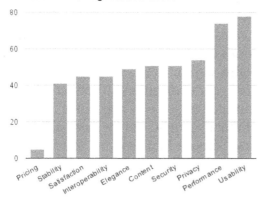

Finance: Average Review Score

Use the category review score averages to get a feeling for which are the easier and the more difficult quality attributes to get right. You can leverage this data if you have a 3-year-old app, or just putting pen to napkin on the next great app. Prioritize design, test and build to make a great app for your category.

See Appendix A for a full listing of review frequencies and scores for all categories.

Applause Quality Score

The method behind the Applause quality score hasn't yet been explained. It is long overdue. The applause team was busy looking into whether the app store reviews were valuable or not. Turns out, I was wrong—I had a verbal bet that the quality of apps over time would be relatively stagnant with little texture. Boy, was I wrong. There was more texture than we could have ever imagined in the review streams. We focused on extracting value from the review stream for app teams to make their apps better—not to manipulate star ratings, or keep track of how many fan bois or haters are out there.

No Ratings: The first major decision in building the applause score was to ignore pure star ratings. Yes, applause scores ignore pure star ratings. If a user says '1 Star'! or '5 Star'!, but leave no text or reasoning, it is not actionable. The product team can't extract any meaningful feedback from that, and if they wanted to, they can easily track their raw star rating in the app stores themselves. The applause scores do tend to be slightly lower than the app store ratings since complainers tend to explain themselves more often than congratulatory Atta boy feedback. Interestingly, this counters the J-Shaped review bias inherent in reviews, so it could be a great thing.

Not Even All Reviews Counted: If reviews don't match one of the common Top 10 quality attributes, they aren't factored into the applause score. Many of these are non-actionable, or random, or incredibly feature-specific. The focus of the applause score was to quantify quality in a way that could enable cross-app comparisons, so they all apps needed to be measured on a common set of attributes. Only about 20% of reviews are filtered out.

Example Reviews that are filtered out of scoring:

Kindle
Books & Reference | Applause Score: 42 100

Review, 5-Star, Kindle, iOS: "Kindle. Book app " -- Kathie Todd

Modern Combat 4: Zero Hour
 Games | Applause Score: 72/100

Review, 5-Star, Modern Combat 4: Zero Hour, iOS: "Buy it. Black ops on your phone, duh " -- Yed ginseng

Potty Time with Elmo
 Education | Applause Score: 35/100

Review, 1-Star, Potty time with Elmo, iOS: "Does not motivate. The app is not well animated. And did not motivate my child. " -- Yed ginseng

Yahoo Finance
 Finance | Applause Score: 64/100

Review, 3-Star, Yahoo Finance, iOS: "I like it. It works " -- Yed ginseng

0-100: To make sure folks don't confuse the applause score with the app store's 5-star ratings; the score is normalized to 0-100. Also, since we give a little extra credit to apps succeeding in important quality areas for their category (see above category data), we end up with numbers that aren't exactly half-star increments.

How it works (from the applause analytics site, written by Rich Weiss):
In the spirit of fairness and transparency, two of Applause's guiding principles, we want to provide a peek behind the scenes to describe how Applause turns big data and complex math into an easily consumed set of actionable scores.

WHAT'S WRONG WITH THE CURRENT STAR RATING APPROACH?

Let's take a look at how an Applause Score stacks up against a star rating in the app stores.

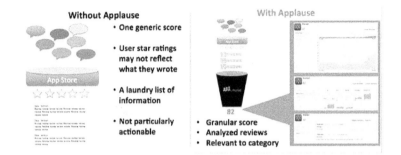

Receiving an app store star-rating of 3.2, a laundry list of reviews, and a simple download count may be okay for a quick snapshot, but it doesn't provide meaningful insights or direction about how to improve your user satisfaction and app quality.

WHERE DID APPLAUSE BEGIN?

We tackled this big data problem by turning loose a team of engineers and data scientists who were formerly at Google and Microsoft. They argued, debated and agonized over this problem for the better part of a year. The result was a lot of sophisticated analysis on the back end, and a decidedly simple way to consume that information. Someone saying 'I like Twitter better' is an opinion, and it is not very useful. But a review that says an app loads slowly compared to similar apps points to something fixable – and important. Look, you can even see some of our early thought process below.

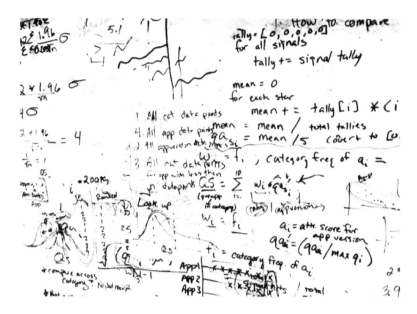

IT'S ALL ABOUT REFINEMENT

So how did we finally arrive at a score that we believe accurately quantifies user satisfaction and the quality of an app, given the imperfect, unstructured nature of the text in user reviews from the different app stores?

To begin, one must understand what data is available to make up an Applause score. Here's how this whole thing works:

- **First, Applause crawls the app stores**. There are new apps and new reviews every day and Applause crawls, and catalogs, mountains of data from the app stores. (1000 EC2 machines for Google Play, because they ironically make it difficult to crawl —Jason)
- **Next, Applause counts and stores the relevant data**. Applause captures basic attributes like App Title, Publisher Name, App Description and Download Counts. But what data really matters when it comes time to quantify app quality and user satisfaction? So while Applause crawls and captures all of the above, it also captures feedback from user reviews. This is where the real magic happens. And because user reviews are not just associated with an app,

but also with the star rating of that review and the specific version of that app, Applause can begin to build a true picture of an app over time and across versions.

Let the quantification begin. Applause analyzes user reviews based on a set of hard-coded attributes that we have discovered embody far-ranging aspects of app quality and user sentiment. How did we get there?

Think of what attributes are important to you when you go to purchase a new home. You might care about the size, the newness, the location, and/or the amenities. Your neighbor might care about a different set of attributes. Each one of these attributes may or may not be useful to you, and, depending upon your circumstances, each may hold a different weight in terms of your buying decision. But these elements are typically relevant to all buyers when making such a purchase. Applause works the same way by providing access to a complete set of attributes.

After forming a hypothesis that included dozens of possible attributes, we let the data prove/disprove them. We discovered ten distinct attributes to help us break down app quality into a more elemental form. They are:

Usability How easy do users find it to navigate and discover the breadth of an app's features?

Security Do users perceive any risk to sign ins, passwords or other sensitive information being vulnerable?

Performance How fast and responsive an app is in standard usage? Does it meet users' expectations?

Stability How often does an app crash, hang or freeze?

Pricing How does an app's perceived value compare with its cost?

Interoperability How well does an app integrates with other services or hardware?

Satisfaction How well does an app satisfy users' core expectations? Is it fun or even healthily addictive to users?

Elegance How attractive, cool or slick is an app's design? Does it cause users to brag about it to their friends?

Privacy How comfortable are users with an app's terms of service and handling of PII? Does the developer live up to the promised terms?

Content How accurate and relevant is an app's data to the user. If the app was localized or translated does it match users' locations and cultures?

1. **More quantification.** Each attribute is triggered by what we call "signals" – keywords that emerge from the data as interesting patterns about particular reviews. For example, keywords like "fast" and "slow" map to the Performance attribute while "captcha" and "sign in" correlate tightly to the Security attribute.
Signals are meant to be neither positive nor negative, they merely act as classifiers for the ten Applause Attributes. Each attribute has between 8 and 17 keyword or key phrase signals mapped to it, for a total of 144 different signals.
2. **Time to bust out the calculators**. Applause begins by counting the number of times it see signals in the reviews for each app version. It then sums these counts up across each attribute and weights them by the respective star rating for each review. This process allows Applause to quantify the impact of a signal on a high or low star rating.
3. **Aggregate data to weight it appropriately**. Before tying everything together, Applause needs to know how much people care about the different attributes. Applause uses the app's category to make that distinction. Applause generates a weight based on the number of signal hits in a particular attribute in each category. For example, in the Financial

app store category users care about Security whereas in the Games category users care more about Performance.

4. **Make the data meaningful by turning it into a number and tying it all together**. Finally Applause multiplies each app's individual Attribute scores by its app store category weight. The resulting products are then averaged to generate the Applause Score, a number between 0 and 100.

WHY ARE WE SO CONFIDENT IN THE NUMBER?

We like big data; we know that bigger data sets yield more accurate results and higher levels of confidence than smaller data sets. And we've also tested and re-tested dozens of versions of our algorithms and weighting formulas over the past several months. Over time, we've continued to refine this process. But in the end, Applause is a tool for business, brand and technical leaders. So we put the Applause Score and Applause Attribute Scores through the ringer, measuring our algorithms against the perceptions of a crowd of software-savvy professionals. These results uncovered exceptions to our rules and sent us back to the lab to further refine. Again and again, we circled this loop until we got to where we are today.

If you're still reading, we'd like to give you a round of applause (pun intended). Let's recap where we are:

- We've stored user sentiments by crawling app stores and saving their associated reviews
- Then we mapped these reviews to a given set of attributes and signals that are relevant
- Finally, we generated a number from 0-100 to help determine the quality of a particular app

BUT WHAT ABOUT APPS WITH SMALL DATA?

We've developed measures to determine the appropriate number of reviews to generate an accurate Applause score. After several iterations we determined that an app must have at least X hits for an attribute and the distribution of the data was within Y variance.

Of course, those numbers are a secret. But rest assured they helped us to determine when there is insufficient data to generate an Applause Score. These apps are be marked by an asterisk within the platform.

HOW TO REPRESENT THE FINAL SCORE

The final decision was to determine if the all-up Applause score for an app should be a score from the most recent version of the app? How about an accumulated score from the past few versions of the app? What about only showing a score where you can trust the data used to generate the score?

We went with the last choice. We worked to maximize the number of apps that would have an Applause score, but also choose a version of the Applause score that would be most reflective of the current app and still be useful to developers. The Applause Score reflects the sentiments of all the users using your app right now. If your score is being dragged down by users of an older build, app owners may want to convince them to update their app. Simply put, a score is a measure of an app's user sentiment today, regardless of the version an individual user is running.

So there you have it folks. Your behind the scenes tour will exit stage left. See you in the gift shop.

Thanks to Rich, who awesomely wears bowties, for providing a very accessible description of the overall applause scoring methodology. Really this is a tool for use to quantify meaningful and actionable quality data from the app store reviews.

It is worth a special note to address the question of social media. Why not also crawl twitter and Facebook posts for feedback on apps? Why just the app store reviews? We investigated this early on. The key issues were:

1. **Fuzzy Mapping to App**: If someone complains about Twitter, on Twitter, are they referring to the app or the web site? It is difficult to tell. Because there isn't a lot of room

for this contextual text in 140 characters. Also, when they do complain about the app, they often fail to mention whether the comment is regarding the iOS or Android app. These are largely to very separate applications, and Twitter has two very different teams working on these apps. Mapping social comments back to the specific app is fuzzy and low confidence, which means it is bad for analytics. With app store reviews, we know it is associated with the exact app and platform they are using.

2. **Fuzzy Sentiment**: Most sentiment analysis engines try to figure out how angry or happy a post is based on the text. These engines often fail with short snippets of text. Give them a paragraph and they are OK. Give these little algorithms 140 characters and they become very unreliable. Also, there is that pesky 'Angry birds is a great game' issue. Most sentiment analysis systems don't recognize that 'Angry' is part of the name of a game, and think the user is very angry about something. Also, posts like "hate this app it is taking all my time and I play it all the time". Well, those get marked as hate, but humans usually interpret this to be a high compliment in the form of sarcasm. With app store reviews, the reviewers leave a little star rating. Social media data is just very fuzzy and we wanted a reliable, predictable system.

In both cases, the app store reviews are far more reliable in terms of sentiment analysis and mapping that comment back to the right app. Social media post analysis sounds great, but is not so great in practice. We even found that humans had about 60% agreement when it came to analyzing the sentiment of social media posts in a casual internal study, which is far from something that we would consider useful. If you have ideas, please let me know, I'd love to see how to use social media with confidence on par with the app store reviews.

Competitive Attribute Analysis

Lets look at how we can use applause scores, per-quality-attribute, to asses how an app is doing versus the competition.

Here we look at four apps: Facebook, Google+, Twitter and LinkedIn. This type of graph is sometimes called a 'radar chart'. Take a second to understand how to read it—it's powerful. Each app is assigned a color, and then each application's score on each of the quality attributes is drawn. If an app is doing very well in an attribute, it will have a 'spike' outward in that part of the graph. The more 'area' an app covers in this graph the better it is doing over all. The smaller the area, the more poorly the app is doing overall. Bigger is better.

Compare: Similarity

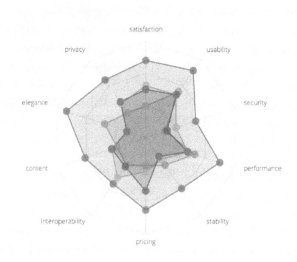

In this radar chart we see that there are many similarities between these social apps—they all have a similar quality attribute 'shape'. Generally speaking, these social networking apps seem to consistently do OK in the areas of performance, usability and satisfaction. But, they also consistently do poorly in the areas of security, privacy, and stability. It is pretty amazing that there is so much consistency between apps that serve similar functions. It likely means that these quality attributes are either particularly easy or difficult for social app teams. It also reflects that users expect very similar things from similar apps.

What if you were twitter looking at this data? The app with redlines in the radar chart above? If you were on the Twitter app team, what would you take away from this radar chart, assuming you felt these other apps were similar?

1. My app is not doing well. I have a small radar footprint across the board—the smallest of this competitive group of apps.
2. It is possible to improve my app's quality in these quality areas. Other apps, that are similar, have better scores. I can't just declare that it is too difficult and move on with feature work.
3. The other apps are relatively 'elegant' compared to their other attribute scores. My app's elegance score is relatively lower than my other attribute scores. This basically means, regardless of absolute quality level, I take far less care in my app's appearance.
4. Many of these attributes, especially stability, are probably easily fixable by detecting and fixing crashes and hangs. I should get on that. We bought a crash collections company, I should talk to them.
5. Hmm, maybe tweets are just a more difficult thing to build an app to support. Maybe Twitter users are just crankier than Facebook or Google+ users. I want to take a look at other twitter clients and see if they are also struggling with the same quality issues since they serve the same market and target users as my official twitter app. Lets look:

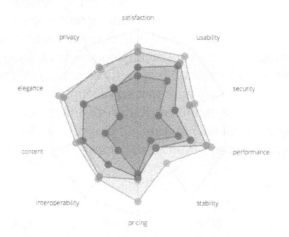

- Yeah, OK, the other twitter apps are awesome on all fronts. I should learn from what they are doing—it really is me.
- It is interesting that in the area of elegance, where my app is the worst, several of these apps have a near perfect elegance scores. It is possible to build a great tweet-based UX and I should try their apps out and see how they do it.
- Stability is also an area where all twitter clients struggle. Perhaps it has something to do with the server/API causing crashes in all the clients? Perhaps this is also a area where if I fix every single crash, the Twitter app can easily beat the competition in the Twitter client world, because there is room to standout on the stability attribute.

Comparison: Difference

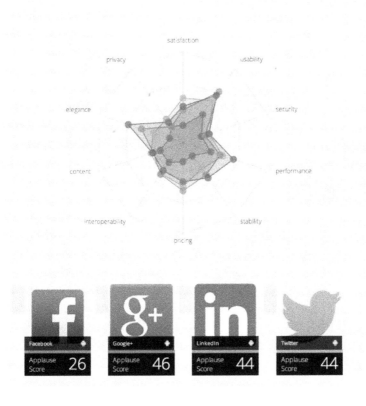

Here we see the same social networking apps, but this is how they match up on the Android platform. It is a much closer quality race on Android, but because they are all of lower quality, not because they are all great apps. Even when two apps seem to have very similar quality attribute scores, you can see some interesting differences and opportunities. In the radar chart above, the four social networking apps on Android are shown with very similar quality 'shapes'. We can see though that the twitter app, again, is relatively 'short' on the elegance leg, both in absolute and relative quality. It is the same story with stability—those two areas should be given special attention on Android as well. Perhaps there are common engineering or design culture issues contributing to the same quality issues across apps. Interestingly, similarities between apps also highlight areas where there is an opportunity to significantly outshine the competition:

- **Easy differentiators**: Here, all social apps seem to have significant issues with security—this is a great opportunity to differentiate the Twitter app from the competition by nailing basic sign in and security perception problems.
- **Some things are just tough**: Where all apps are doing poorly together, is also an indication that this might just be a difficult quality attribute to get right. App teams can gain some solace in the fact that everyone else struggles with these quality areas too

Platform: Differences

If we compare the iOS and the Android radar charts above, for the same four social networking apps, we see there are significant differences between the platforms. Not all platforms, or apps on different platforms are created equal. Here we can see that users are generally less happy with these four social networking apps on Android than they are for those same social networking apps on iOS. Different approaches are needed to address quality issues on specific platforms.

The Category Level

It is easy to get caught up in comparing a single app to directly competitive apps. But, it is also worth noting where these apps compare against the larger app category they live in. For this example, lets look at some shopping apps: Amazon, Staples, and Walmart. It is an interesting mix. Amazon is the incumbent online retailer, with a large mobile investment in its apps and Kindle platform. Walmart has joined the high-stakes app retail battle by building out a large team of talented engineers they call Walmart Labs. Walmart has built their team lightning quick through acquisitions of mobile app startups, and they work out of the former YouTube offices near San Francisco, and another office in Portland. Staples, is another, more specialized, retail giant with a strong web presence, trying to enter the app world. Lets take a peek at how their apps are doing competitively against each other, but in the larger context of all apps in the same category.

Here is a chart showing the applause scores for Amazon, Walmart and Staples, and where they fit within the larger distribution of app scores in the iOS lifestyle category (the category where these apps are deployed). You can see that Amazon and Walmart are neck-and-neck, with staples a distant third, in overall app quality. But, what is important to see here is that there are many apps in the lifestyle category with far better app scores. This means that Amazon should realize that they might be winning a close race with Walmart, but it might be losing the overall quality race. There are probably a few things that all three companies could learn by looking at all these other lifestyle apps that are bringing in really great reviews from their users.

Next we see the same chart of these three shopping giants with Amazon leading Walmart by a bit wider margin, and staples further behind. Again, both Walmart and Amazon still have quite a ways to go to be at the head of this category (shopping on Android).

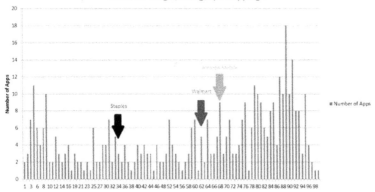

Distribution of Applause Scores
Market: Google, Category: Shopping

If you squint at the chart you will notice that the height of these graphs represent the number of apps that have a given applause score—the higher the bar in the graph, the more apps that share that score. The distribution shows that these three apps not only have about '40' points worth of quality to improve, but there are many apps ahead of them (to the right) in terms of user happiness.

Here is another view of these three apps, but focusing on the score of a single quality attribute: usability. Overall, averaged across all quality attributes, the race might be tight between Amazon and Walmart, but you can see that if you look at just the usability feedback, is Amazon is losing this race. More importantly, you can see here that, again, many apps have far better usability than either app in the larger picture. Note: The spike at 100 is for many small apps that have very few, but consistently perfect usability feedback.

Distribution of Usability Scores
Market: Apple, Category: Lifestyle

Distribution of Ship Frequency

Lets now look at some indication of how 'agile' or 'lean' these app teams appear to be based on how frequently they release new versions. We see a chart that shows the number of different app versions that Amazon, Walmart and Staples have released. Apps that ship many different versions are on the right; apps that have shipped very few versions are on the left. Notice also that many apps have shipped only one version, and the number of apps (the size of the bars) that have shipped more than one version drops off quickly. Very few apps ship as many times as Amazon has --27 separate versions. Walmart has released 19 versions, and Staples only 11 at the time of this writing. One app has even shipped 64 times. There seems to be anecdotal data that correlation between shipping frequently, a hallmark of agile and lean teams, leads to higher quality—we'll investigate that more below.

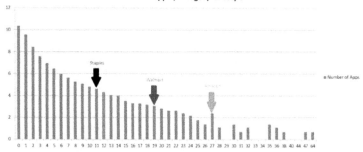

Distribution of Number of Versions
Market: Apple, Category: Lifestyle

App Quality: Secrets for Agile App Teams

Agile Quality Myth

Proponents of Agile or Lean methodologies often assume that shipping frequently improves the quality of their apps. Shipping frequently and iterating is all the rage if you read tech blogs or go to conferences. The applause team set out to see if the app store data backed this theory up. If we could show that all this hype was real, we might be invited to more agile conferences.

Using the millions of apps and the hundreds of millions of reviews applause.com has in its index; we went looking for a correlation between shipping early and often and leveraging star ratings as proxy for app quality.

Number of App Versions vs. Star Rating

The first attempt to find a correlation between agile and app quality was to look to see if apps that had many different versions over the past year showed better star ratings than those with fewer versions.

Using the same top 1000 apps in the app store, the x-axis is the star rating and the y-axis is the number of versions the app has published. The Pearson correlation is -0.28, which is below the threshold for showing a significant correlation. No dice. Keep believing, but there is no data indicating that lean or agile methodologies are leading to better apps.

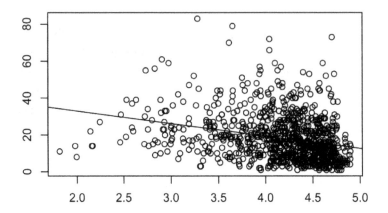

Number of Days Since Release vs. Star Rating

Dismayed at the prospect of no conference trips this year, at least no paid trips, the team looked for another way to hunt down any evidence of agile or lean methodologies having an impact on star quality. This chart shows the correlation between number of days since release and star rating. The thought being that if apps are released often and/or more recently, they will be of higher quality. Probably not so, says the data. At best, the data is definitely not conclusive. It might just be biased by the fact that apps released more recently were built with better tooling, or don't suffer from looking 'old'. There is a weak, very weak, correlation here. Nothing to call home about.

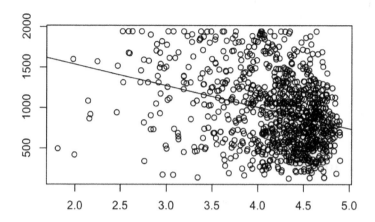

The x-axis is the star rating. The y-axis is the number of days since the current version was released. The Pearson correlation is -0.31, where the threshold for weak/medium correlation is 0.3). The apps selected here are the top 1000 apps that have more than 10,000 reviews. If you don't know what the Pearson number is, don't worry, it is a data-nerd term, and you can read more on Wikipedia. Note, the same calculation was done across all apps, not just the top 1000 apps, which showed the same weak correlation. We tried the same calculation on only 'top' apps in the effort to filter out possible noise from little used or one off hobby-apps that might not be backed by teams professionally or seriously engaged in agile or lean methodologies.

We tried to find strong evidence that all the agile and lean startup stuff is working. We tried. The good news in all this…there is likely very little fundamental risk in switching to an agile model from an app quality perspective.

Summary of Quality versus Ship frequency

In the end, the data seems to show that shipping frequently because it is the hip thing to do, doesn't mean your app will necessarily be a better app. Anecdotally, after talking with many top app development and test teams, and project managers that oversee hundreds of mobile app test cycles, it appears that the critical difference between great apps and so-so apps simply comes down to caring about quality. Too often, app teams are focusing on adding features as fast as possible, and often ignoring the backlog of known crashes and user complaints. If there was a single way to summarize app quality today, much has changed, but much has remained the same—app teams that care about quality over features make better apps.

Mobile vs. Native Quality

There is a lot of discussion these days about whether app teams should build native or hybrid apps. Sometimes a picture is worth a 1000 words. Look at the following chart of Facebook's iOS app quality. Can you tell when the Facebook app team re-wrote their hybrid app as a native app? Other apps have shown similar quality bumps when they migrated to a native design. Based on the data, I always recommend a native app unless you just can't afford it, and the team and company and brand is OK with having a lower quality app.

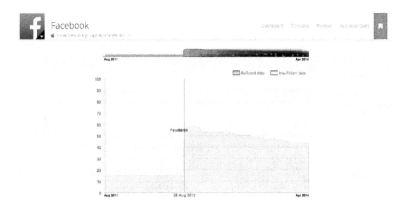

Section IV: Test Automation

"The smartest developer on your team should be the one writing your tests."
— Simon Stewart, a core member of the Selenium team at Google, and now at Facebook.

Test automation is like all political issues; there are several camps with huge bias. PM's and testers with little programming experience are sometimes intimidated by automation. Engineers, especially engineers only a few years out of school, think automation will solve the world's problems. Sometimes this bias also comes from previous experiences such as successful software companies that saw great success with little automation, or those that have seen highly efficient test-driven development teams that needed no manual or user testing. As with most politics, the correct answer usually lies somewhere in the middle, is nuanced, and "depends". If you peek at someone's resume, you can likely predict their feelings on test automation without talking to them.

A few questions can quickly identify if, and how much, you should invest in test automation:

Q: Are you a bank? Does your app deal with money? Do people's lives depend on your app? **Automate**. You should be building a full suite of regression automation for your app.

Q: Does your app simply show data pulled from your website? Is it a simple newsreader? **No need to automate** unless most of your business, engagement, or money flows through the app.

Q: Is your app experimental? Are you still looking for product-market fit? **Don't automate yet;** wait until you know what you are building. Automating now will distract from iterating on the product, and much of your code would likely be thrown away as you iterate on your design before you got a return on your automation investment.

Q: Is your app valuable independent of a website? Are you a hot new mobile messaging startup flirting with a $30M or $2B valuation? **Automate a bit**. It will keep you from experiencing a dramatic FAIL, and make you look semi-professional to investors and any due diligence from potential acquirers.

Q: Do you work at an old school software company where the only road to promotion in the testing organization is to show that you can write some code? **Automate until you get promoted, then stop.**

Q: Is it an app for an internal, small (<1000) person audience? Is critical to your sales force to demonstrate your companies' value to prospects while on the road? Could your app's failure mean an indirect loss of revenue or sales? **Automate a bit.** When your app does eventually fail, the witch-hunt will ask this question. Not that automation would have prevented it, but it looks like you performed due-diligence during the post mortem.

Q: Is your app 'done'? Do you expect your app to enter 'maintenance mode' soon? **Automate a little bit** so you don't have to worry about it.

Q: Do you have daily or hourly app builds? Does your team practice 'Continuous Integration' (CI)? **Automate as much as you can bear.** To reap the full benefit of continuous integration, you need to catch bugs as soon as they occur, and only automation will be fast enough to catch most regressions before the next build. If you catch the bug quickly in a CI environment it is far easier to isolate the offending code check-in because there are so few new ones in each build.

When in doubt, most app teams should eventually automate a basic set of test, but only a few. Only build extensive tests after you know the app, in its current form, is going to be important.

The calculus for test automation in the world of mobile apps is significantly different than for traditional web or desktop apps. There are many factors to both motivate and suppress investments in the app world:

Speed Causes Breaks: The mobile world is typically faster-paced with more design and functional iterations, meaning there is less time to reap the rewards for investing in automation—your tests often fail because the product changed, not because they found a bug.

Opportunity Cost: Anyone capable of writing test automation could likely be writing features in your app. There is a shortage of mobile app developers today, so even when you do invest in some programming testers, they are often quickly lured away to work on important new features or bugs fixes within your company, and more often, lured straight to other companies.

Speed Means No Time: The speed of agile and continuous integration environments means that time is at a premium. If you have a new build every hour, the only way you will know if the build is good or bad is by having some automation running—you don't have time between builds to wait for manual testing.

Immature Infrastructure: Test automation infrastructure is still maturing today. Until recently many frameworks were either platform-specific (didn't support both Android and iOS), only ran on simulators or only on real devices, or were closed-source proprietary systems that you shouldn't bet on long term.

The hottest of political discussions in quality engineering is often around which test framework to use. The spectrum of frameworks, with their various plusses and minuses, is wide and deep. I've evaluated many of these frameworks, and can only recommend a single test framework as of this writing (and, I couldn't have recommended it at all 6 months ago). I'll leave the biased and often ill-informed test framework debates to the blogs and stackoverflow.com.

appium

Appium is frankly the best of the mediocre set of options today. It has all the benefits and downfalls of being a derivative of selenium—the biggest name in web test automation. Even though it has a complex protocol, and requires the device to be tethered to the driver and cannot run standalone inside the client, its advantages far outweigh the negatives. The significant advantages are cross-platform, familiar API and model for engineers transitioning from web test automation, open source, runs on both simulators and real-world hardware, and maintained by the community and smart folks at SauceLabs.com who will even execute the tests for you. Appium also has the advantage of libraries for most major programming languages.

Here is a video of Appium in action: http://goo.gl/Ps8La7

I would advise the against hipster rush to use the cucumber/calabash stack. Nine months ago, it was the state of the art, but in particular, the use of cucumber in a mobile environment is dangerously expensive in the real-world of agile app teams. Cucumber promises that you can write an abstraction layer for basic app actions, and then let non-programmers create the test scripts and validation by composing these basic actions and validations. Avoiding the larger discussion of whether non-programmers should be writing test automation scripts, the fundamental weakness is that app teams are changing their UX and functionality very quickly. The end result is often tests that have false positives, and a team of testers that can't debug why the test script failed—or fix it. It looks great on paper, but be cautious. I've run into many former calabash and cucumber fans.

The one test framework that had the strengths that Selenium is missing was KIF, from the clever folks at Square.com, which processes mobile payments via phones, who knew test automation was critical important for their app. They knew it was important because their app processes money and is the core to the business flow of company. Magically simple, KIF can run independent of a controller machine, has full access to the internals of the app—because it lives inside the app build—no state or event is out of its reach of its automation. KIF suffers in every other respect though as it is iOS specific, and most notably, only developers can really be expected to write tests with it. But like Simon says...maybe that's the way it should be.

If you are only focusing on a single platform, Android or iOS, and aren't overly interested in leveraging the same test logic across both platforms, Robotium for Android and UIAutomation for iOS are the de-facto standards and work very well. Robotium is open source and supports testing both native and hybrid apps and the tests are written in Java. UIAutomation test scripts for iOS apps are written in JavaScript. Both frameworks drive the application by driving the app's UI elements with clicks and gestures. This sometimes requires testers to ask their developers to add extra annotations to make the application fully testable. Both frameworks test from the outside-in, where KIF tests from the inside out. That means these frameworks can do most everything a user can do, but test developers will have trouble measuring internal application state for validation, and the speed of test execution can be slower driving the UX versus the underlying applications APIs. Overall, these are good, and safe, bets for automation but make sure you won't wish you had a cross platform automation solution like Appium later.

Section V: Putting it all Together

Great, we've covered lots of data, tips and tricks, but how does all this applied to real world app design, programming, and testing? We'll look at applying these tips and tricks, data and tools to a real world app or two. Armed with all this data, we can build a pretty solid quality plan without even working on the app team itself—that's the power of app stores and data.

1. **Data Gathering**
    a. Quality over time
    b. Basic quality attribute analysis
    c. Most common feedback
    d. Competitive Analysis
    e. Category Baseline
    f. Cross-Platform
2. **Planning**
    a. Prioritizing the data
    b. Getting basic bugs out of the way
    c. Incorporating feedback and wish lists
    d. Test: Apply Quality Attribute and App Tips
    e. Development: Apply Quality Attribute and App Tips
    f. Product and Design: Apply Quality Attribute and App Tips
3. **Executing**
    a. Measuring build over build quality

1a: Quality over time

To have a 5-star app, you need to know where you stand, and what is fixable. Every day that passes is another day collecting poor reviews that are with your app forever. Lets use analytics.applause.com since it was designed for this very task. Lets use the Quip app as an example of an upstart app, with a very smart team, going up against well-funded competitors. Its core function, a word processor, is familiar to everyone, and there aren't a million reviews (yet!) to consider, so it is a well-scoped app for a short section in a book on app quality.

For those not familiar with Quip, it is a document editor with a strong focus on collaboration and a mobile app friendly UX. Why look at Quip? Some parts of this book were written in Quip, so it is on the mind, and about anyone can relate to the quality issues a document-editing app might have. Take a quick look at Quip's own description of their app:

"Quip is a modern word processor that enables you to create beautiful documents on any device, including the iPad, iPhone, and the desktop. It combines documents and messages into a single chat-like "thread" of updates — making collaboration easy.

Take notes, organize to-do lists, and collaborate within your company. Share folders to organize your projects at home or at work. All features work perfectly offline, syncing whenever you have an Internet connection.

Key Features:

• Real-time, collaborative editing
• Messaging - Every document has a chat thread
• Offline - Edit anywhere, even on an airplane
• Folders - Share with your family or team
• Checklists - Interactive, shared lists
• Diffs - Every edit is in a document news feed
• Presence - See who's online, what they're up to
• @mentions - Link to people and documents
• Notifications - Know when a doc is opened
• Read receipts - Check who's read your edits
• Inbox - See what you haven't read

Quip also works on the desktop (Mac and PC). Access anywhere at http://quip.com."

Quip

By Quip

Open iTunes to buy and download apps.

View In iTunes

This app is designed for both iPhone and iPad.

Free

Category: Productivity
Updated: Mar 20, 2014
Version: 1.7
Size: 12.0 MB
Languages: English, Chinese, French, German, Italian, Japanese, Portuguese, Russian,

View More by This Developer

Description

Quip is a modern word processor that enables you to create beautiful documents on any device, including the iPad, iPhone, and the desktop. It combines documents and messages into a single chat-like "thread" of updates — making collaboration easy.

Take notes, organize to-do lists, and collaborate within your company. Share folders to organize your projects at home or at work. All features work perfectly offline, syncing whenever you have an internet connection.

Key Features:

- Real-time collaborative editing
- Messaging – Every document has a chat thread
- Offline – Edit anywhere, even on an airplane
- Folders – Share with your family or team
- Checklists – Interactive, shared lists
- Diffs – Every edit is in a document news feed
- Presence – See who's online, what they're up to
- @mentions – Link to people and documents
- Notifications – Know when a doc is opened
- Read receipts – Check who's read your edits
- Inbox – See what you haven't read

Quip also works on the desktop (Mac and PC). Access anywhere at http://quip.com

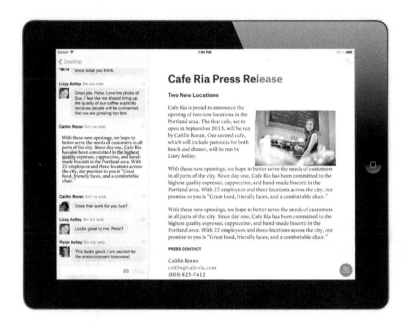

(images from http://quip.com)

Now that everyone is introduced to Quip, lets take a quick look at Quip's current review feedback summary data.

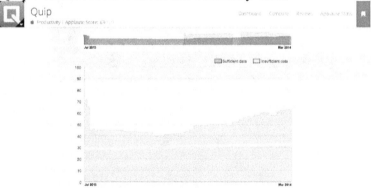

Here we see Quip's user sentiment over time. Good news, it looks like the early adopters (and their friends and family were pretty enamored with the initial release). Then, as is typical with apps, users had more time to acclimate to the app, find bugs, and that started a quick drop quality sentiment. Then, Quip began a series of quality and feature improvements over several release cycles. We can see here that their cadence of release has slowed a bit (the orange dots at the top represent dates when a new version was deployed). Perhaps the team is focusing more on quality and incorporating feedback, or distracted building their Android app. The app feels healthy, looks like the team is focusing on quality, but still has room to improve. Most apps have a general downward trend, so you can tell that the team has been doing some great quality work as the trend is up and to the right.

1B: Basic quality attribute analysis

Now lets take look at the specific quality attributes that impact the overall score. Which attributes are going well and which are going poorly?

These quality attribute scorecards show as red if the app is scoring below the average attribute score for that category. If you are paying attention, you will notice that only 6 of the 10 quality attributes are shown here. The missing four are due to the lack of a large number of reviews in those areas since the app is relatively new. Also, a couple attributes have very divergent texture of reviews (lots of 1's and 5's or all over the place), meaning we can't yet tell what the true user sentiment has converged yet. The average score for apps in this app category is shown on the graph as the little grey line. Lets start with the good stuff:

Satisfaction. Quip's users are super happy with the app. They love it. Recommending it. And, even when they run into an issue the support team takes care of them. All great examples of how to ensure your app has happy users.

Review, 5-Star, Quip, iOS: "Fantastic Simple Software. When I have time I will write a through review but I strongly recommend getting Quip. " – Vic Healey

Review, 5-Star, Quip, iOS: "My wife and I love it! We use it for sharing all sorts of lists. Serious stuff, fun stuff, etc. It's awesome. " – Edward E Nigma

Review, 5-Star, Quip, iOS: "Great. Had a glitch on this app. I contacted the support team and was helped quickly and effectivly. This is my favorite app for writing ideas, resumes, anything really. " – PJPotamus

Review, 5-Star, Quip, iOS: "Has a few bugs but an overall outstanding product. When I say bugs, I mean there were a *lot* of bugs in the beginning. Basic functions like copy/paste, insert, etc. didn't work correctly. Luckily the Quip team has been improving that and there are very few noticeable bugs now. That said, this is a great app. I seriously use it for everything text-related (usually I use the in-browser version, but when I'm on the go I use the app). I love the font, and I love the auto-formatting. Sometimes I used to spend hours reformatting stuff I would copy from the internet or from e-books, etc., but it is painless now. It is extremely simple, and that's what's made me migrate nearly all my documents from my computer to Quip. It is on Quip that I do my best thinking because it makes the whole formatting part so effortless, it provides a great user interface, and it lets me organize my thoughts like never before. I would highly recommend this app. That said, I suppose it is only for a certain subset of people. " – Vaniificat

Performance is another great quality attribute for Quip. Their users are crowing about how fast this app performs. Performance is an especially tough attribute for any client/server app. Here are some representative reviews about performance:

Review, 5-Star, Quip, iOS: "Fast, easy to use. Best mobile co-editing and sharing app.Freakin fast. " – Jacky Wang

Review, 5-Star, Quip, iOS: "Super fast and easy! No nonsense app " – Arsenal777

Now lets get to the attributes that could still use some TLC.

Content

Ads, incorrect data, or content download issues can seriously affect users perception of app quality.

Based on 15 reviews

Content: Remember, the content attributes relates to bad data, input, output, data loss, and download problems. Looks like Quip users are having issues with getting their content into Quip (lack of import from many popular sources), and exporting of content (only output format being PDF until recently), and a note about possible data loss when copying anything but basic text into the app, and lack of expected content formatting features. The Quip team may have even deliberately avoided fancy formatting features in the interest of simplicity—but this is an example where you can't control your user base's expectations. If the average user expects your app to have certain features—they will complain about it, feel dissatisfied and post negative reviews that could deter your core user base. The awesome thing here is that the users are telling Quip exactly what features they want and need to make Quip a better app, and avoid future negative reviews in this app quality attribute.

Review, 2-Star, Quip, iOS: "Great but limited export. Quip is elegant and the collaboration feature works great. I'd like a few more text formatting options but nothing critical. Unfortunately the only export option is PDF (or copy/paste I suppose) which unfortunately means I can't use it. " – StupendousMan

Review, 1-Star, Quip, iOS: "Missing paragraph? I wrote an important letter and a paragraph is gone. Just like that ? " – Mr Naji

Update: While finishing up this book, the quip team seems to have

listened to users and released support for synchronizing docs with
box.net and Dropbox.com for better content and interoperability
with other apps.

Interoperability Quip's negative interoperability feedback is
focused on interaction with the operating system's clipboard
functionality, the screen blanking out (perhaps Quip can avoid the
device diming on readers?), and more comments about exporting
the content so they can use the documents they created in other
apps via email integration.

Review, 1-Star, Quip, iOS: "Useless! The screen often blanks
out. Tables can't be adjusted (column width). Unreliable. Does not
link up to Google in spite of its claims. Getting to the desktop on
my iPhone is often impossible. Good potential but needs lots of
work to be usable. " – AT hiker

Review, 5-Star, Quip, iOS: "Great app for collaboration. Does an
excellent job with syncs/merges. The integration of chat is great
and notifications are spot on. " – iPhone iJunkie

Review, 2-Star, Quip, iOS: "Great potential, not ready yet. App
fails in two crucial ways: input and output. Input (import) is
limited to cut and paste, and it doesn't do that very well. It could
not directly handle a text list in mail with non-alphabetical
characters like the copyright symbol: it pasted nothing. I had to
paste to another notes app, and copy and paste again. That lost all

carriage returns. Output is limited to copy and paste, or a mailed PDF. It would be nice to be able to delete messages too. I hope it improves, but I can't use it yet. It is probably not quite the tool I want, but it could grow into it. " – Quark Gluon Plasma

Stability isn't one of the highlights of Quip's quality. From the average, grey line in the Stability attribute card, we can see that stability in this app category is difficult, and quip isn't too far from the average, but there is lots of room to improve here. The app is simply crashing too often for too many folks.

Review, 1-Star, Quip, iOS: "Crashy. Simply doesn't work. Crashes galore. Also annoying to have to sign in with Google. " – Henry Junior

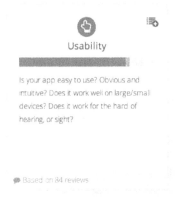

Usability is an interesting example of where Quip is doing well but could still use some work. Quip's usability score is slightly below the average for usability in this category, but it doesn't have much room to improve. Generally folks say the app is very usable, even for new users and love the simplicity of Quip's UX. Specifically folks are looking for more detailed control over their document layout, and there are some usability issues and confusion around folder creation and access. The Quip team should be proud of their powerful and minimal UX, but also focus on these usability nits to improve their users happiness with usability.

Review, 4-Star, Quip, iOS: "Elegant, powerful. For me, simple + powerful = elegant. With Quip:- Writing is clear & uncluttered. Elegant and enjoyable.- Collaboration is simple and powerful.- Organization is clean & simple. The best metaphor for me is: Quip is to the conscious mind what Evernote is to the unconscious. Meaning, I use Quip for things I'm actually going to focus on - particularly for writing. Evernote stores heaps of stuff - all sorts of articles and bookmarks and recipes and photos and whatever else - but it is not efficient to access that storehouse for the things I write in daily (or nearly so). Similarly, it would nullify the elegance of Quip to store ALL my digital stuff in there (just like we luckily cannot keep everything in our minds in our attention at one time); it is most useful for that which I give my attention to on a regular basis.I'll be looking to use Quip in more contexts (besides journaling, note-taking and dreamlining), such as with teams. I hope Quip can make the interconnection between its service and other services (GDrive, Dropbox, Evernote, etc.) more useful." – Reader980127

Review, 4-Star, Quip, iOS: "Elegant, intuitive, snappy, powerful. It's occasionally a bit buggy (but not catastrophic yet).I don't like it asking permission to modify my gmail contacts (so I used a non-gmail email).I'd like more versioning or backup features, and exporting to more editable formats (not just PDF)." -- JimQ9

Review, 4-Star, Quip, iOS: "Confusing navigation but great collaborative editing

Folder interface is non-intuitive (where is that folder i just made?) but the collaborative editing works very well. Only real gripe is the lack of Markdown support." -- tecto

1C: Most common feedback

Now lets dig into what users are commonly saying about specific aspects of Quip. For that, we look at reviews that are saying similar things. Analytics.applause.com can auto group (aka cluster) similar reviews. But, Quip doesn't have enough reviews for that to work well. Lesson here is that the more downloads an app has, the more reviews it has, the more data it has to make smarter app quality decisions. We'll peek at an app with enough reviews to cluster later.

1D: Competitive Analysis

The competition: Lets see how Quip is stacking up against directly competitive apps. Here is the magic 'radar' chart showing how well Quip compares, quality attribute for quality attribute. Remember, bigger is better. Quip only has a six attributes, versus the ten possible, given how few reviews it has to date. This radar chart only has six axes, because we can't compare what we can't measure yet. Specifically, lets compare Quip with Apple's Pages app (on its home turf of iOS), and Microsoft Word, and IA Writer (also focused on minimal and mobile-first UX, like Quip):

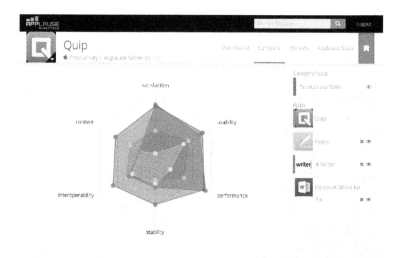

Radar charts, also called 'spiderweb charts' by some people, can give you amazing insights, but you have to stare at them a bit to understand what they are trying to tell you. What we see here is each app's "quality web", stretched across these shared six attributes: Content, interoperability, stability, performance, usability and satisfaction. Each app has its own color. Quip (blue), Pages (orange), IA Writer (red), and Microsoft Word (yellow). Each quality attribute line starts at the center and extends outward to the edge. The center is a zero score for that attribute. If the app is doing well in that attribute its web will be stretched out further from the edge along that axis.

At a glance we can see that Microsoft Word, the web of connected yellow dots is very small. This tells us that overall quality sentiment is very poor. Microsoft Word's satisfaction score is amazingly low (a quick look shows many reviews complaining bout how expensive the app is, and how many features it lacks). Much the same can be of Apple's Pages app—though they seem to be doing better with the content attribute as it as stronger support for copy paste and formatting than does Quip today. We can see here that Quip is doing very well in terms of user sentiment versus two entrenched, rich, and massive competitors, which is great news for the team. The smaller rival Quip has happier users across most quality attributes than the entrenched competition. The team should take some pride in that.

On the other end of the spectrum, we see that IA Writer has a larger web (red) than Quip's (blue). There is interesting texture to the data. IA Writer and Quip are near equals when it comes to the attributes of usability, performance, and satisfaction. What does it mean to the Quip team that a similar app is doing far better in the attributes of stability, interoperability and content? It means someone else building a similar product is doing better on those attributes, so it is possible for them to do better as well. The Quip team should review IA Writers features and reviews, as they relate to interoperability and content. The Quip team should be using the IA Writer app and see how it deals with copy/paste, import and export, and learn from what that app is doing well. As an example, it IA Writer seems to have a 'copy to' feature that their users love.

Review, 5-Star, IA Writer, iOS: "Good for focus on first drafts Bare bones, helps you focus. Great keypad. Has become my go-to choice for first drafts. Usually I use the "copy text" feature to bring the finished draft into another app like pages for formatting. For a longer work, I write chapters or scenes first in iawriter, then put them into the bigger structure of the book and revise in storyist. Dropbox sync is great, too." – Philm36

It looks that less might be more, even for Quip. IA Writer's users tend to love the simplicity, and the expectation, of not even adding images. Something for Quip to consider? Or, perhaps make the image features so simple or magical that it is a competitive advantage vs IA Writer.

Review, 5-Star, IA Writer, iOS: "Focused, No Frills I have Pages, Notes, and Evernote in addition to iA Writer and iA Writer has been the one that has made typing on my iPad focused, simple and easy. I do all rough drafts on iA Writer before importing them into WordPress for editing and publishing. iA Writer makes typing a rough draft pleasant by avoiding anything but the most basic tools needed so that you can focus on writing and worry about adding pictures, and other formatting later when you import it into a different program." -- Ross Walline

1E: Category Baseline

Now, lets look at Quip's category for clues as to which quality attributes are most talked about, and which are the toughest. Quip is listed in the app store in the productivity category. Lets peek at this category's stats (from Appendix A):

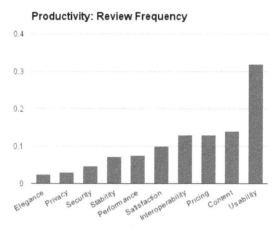

When it comes to the productivity app category, users overwhelmingly talk about one attribute in particular, usability, followed by three others: content, pricing, and interoperability. Review frequency is important to note because it drives the app store ratings and reveals what quality issues users care about most. Reviews in these areas will overly influence the app's final app store average star rating so it is critical for Quip to excel in these quality areas. In the case of the productivity category, app reviews regarding usability are far more likely to impact your star rating for good (or bad). What does this mean for Quip? It is great that Usability is a strong suit, but there is still room to improve in this area, which means there is still upside to their star ratings. The quip team seems to be focusing on the most important quality issue for the productivity category. But, looking at the next 3 most important attributes we see a problem. Pricing isn't a significant attribute for quip as is it free, for good or bad. But, Content and Interoperability are two attributes where Quip is suffering. This means that all things being equal, the Quip team should probably shift attention to quality issues in these two areas before looking further into new features, or usability and stability issues.

Productivity: Average Review Score

Now lets analyze the average review scores for apps in this category across the various quality attributes. We immediately see that most productivity apps score well in usability--one of Quips strong points. While it is great that Quip is doing well in usability, it also means less since we know that most productivity apps also do well in this area. We can see that Quip's two problem attributes, interoperability and content are low scoring in this category, but Quip is still below the average. This means those two are tough areas for productivity apps, so the Quip team should expect that a lot of effort is needed to excel in these areas.

It is also noteworthy that users aren't generally all that happy with productivity apps. This is likely due to expectation of users coming from more fully featured desktop apps with mice and keyboards. Quip rocks in this category with a much higher satisfaction score than most apps in this category. Satisfaction is as much about market-fit and brand, as it is functional quality and design—this might be helping Quip's overall sentiment quite a bit. We've seen how Quip compares to direct competitors. Here we can see another radar chart showing how Quip stacks up against the average of all apps in the productivity category:

Relative to the general expectations of productivity apps, Quip (blue) is doing slightly better than average (grey) in satisfaction and performance, and on-par in terms of usability. Quip has a ways to go in terms of interoperability and content, as we learned above, and they can feel close to average in terms of stability. Regarding stability, we can see here that being excellent in this attribute might mean a significant relative quality advantage versus other apps in this category—if the Quip team dug its heels in and caught and fixed every crash and freeze it had, they might rocket past of the competition in terms of overall user happiness.

1F: Platform Specific

Like many apps these days, Quip ships apps on both Android and iOS. We've been looking at their iOS app. Given that the Android and iOS apps have basically the same goal, same design ethos, and likely using the same server backend and APIs, comparing an app with its twin on another platform can be a good way to isolate platform or team-specific issues. To all you nerds paying rapt attention out there, yes, the analysis has shown that the average satisfaction and attribute scores are about the same, per-category, across app stores these days now that the market has matured, so that's not a significant source of bias. Comparing the same app across app stores can yield some basic insights. Lets peek at another radar chat comparing Quip's iOS and Android apps with each other:

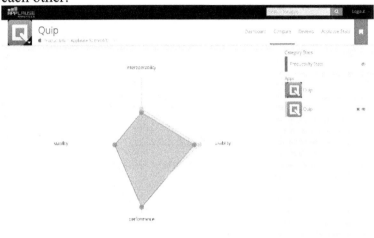

Quip's Android app is even newer than their iOS app, has fewer reviews, thus comparison across only 4 quality attributes is possible. The data looks somewhat like we'd expect—they have a similar shape. Many apps, cross platform, have similar 'radar' profiles, which lends anecdotal credence to the fact that this analysis is really quantifying and capturing the texture of app-specific user quality sentiments. Getting back to the analysis, Quip, on Android, seems slightly less stable. At least Quip's iOS developers have bragging rights at lunch, but after lunch they should both get back to fixing their stability issues. But the Android folks can claim that their app has had less time to bake in production. Both teams could probably benefit from many of the tips in the stability attribute section above.

2A: Prioritizing the data

Lets start applying what we've learned to Quip. The most critical quality attributes in terms of category importance, where Quip is behind the competition, and has the most to gain from improvements are content, interoperability, and a distant third is stability. Remember that the stability attribute isn't relatively as important in this app category, and that the category average for stability was also very low. Stability is important, just not quite the expected return on investment as in the other two quality areas. Content and interoperability are both areas where users are chatty in the app store, where Quip is suffering quality issues, and where we know it is possible to achieve high quality thanks to IA Writer.

2B: Getting basic bugs out of the way

First things first, the Quip team should fix the bugs reported in app store reviews that match these top priority quality attributes. For brevity in this book, we'll highlight a few from the reviews listed above:

Content + Interoperability
Copy/Paste text containing special characters
Possible issue with screen blanking during us
Bug with syncing with Google Docs (or user education issue)
Triple check every place where possible data loss could occur (networking, multi-client syncing, etc.)

Stability
Every crash stack trace is an automatic bug. On Android, there are specific mentions of crashing on launch and when switching between apps.

This bug list should likely be Quip's next sprint. A quality-focused engineering sprint is a great thing. These are issues are severe enough that it is tough to imagine other app feature work that should come before these bug fixes.

2C: Incorporating user feedback and wish lists

You can see that users are giving strong feedback as to the features they are missing and wishing for.

Content

Support additional fonts and text formatting

Ability to adjust table and layout with more precision/control

Interoperability

Export to more formats than PDF

Integration with Box.net/Dropbox.com Note: As of publishing time, the Quip team rolled out support for both Box and Dropbox…maybe they are listening to their review stream).

It is likely that all these features are on Quip's radar for the future. in their backlog, but they should fix them immediately to take care of their users and avoid any more of these reviews piling up for posterity. App teams often feel the rush to get to market. The lean-startup methodology tells folks to ship a minimum viable product (MVP) and keep iterating—in the days of app stores, that's flirting with danger. Users expect a minimum of functionality and when it is missing, they will complain, and it is part of your app's review history forever. The app stores don't let Quip to target only "early adopters", so users pick up the app expecting a fully features competitor to Apple's Pages app. Still, following the lean and agile models, user feedback should be high when prioritizing the next set of features—most teams don't really do that in practice. At the time of writing there were no negative app store reviews regarding the ability to comment, but the Quip team just delivered a major release with awesome commenting functionality and support for Word Press export—despite the fact that a quick scan doesn't show any one- or two- star reviews asking for either of these features. Perhaps there are more strategic motivations in their feature planning, but from a quality-, agile- and lean-perspective, it might be best to focus on the features users are requesting publicly in the app store reviews—before they pile up.

2D: Test: Apply Quality Attribute and App Tips

From above, we know that content, interoperability and stability need some TLC. Lets look at the relevant tips for these attributes and quality monsters (listed in detail far above). It appears that Quip could use more testing in these recommended areas:

Quality Attribute Content
App Breeze: Focus on content freshness. Make sure it takes little or no time to load up a folder list and documents. Quip is fast, but it is still not 'instant on'. Perhaps leveraging notifications to force quip to update local document caches would be useful if it doesn't overly drain the battery or burden the network.

Retentive Specifically look for any way to induce data loss and fix it. Add test cases that simultaneously update the same section of the same document on all clients. Generate test cases for scenarios where the user is moving focus around and hitting the backspace key. Perhaps focus in a document can be off-screen when the delete button is clicked, so the user doesn't notice she has deleted some text, and then later blames Quip for losing data. This is a rich area, and even the appearance or inadvertent loss of data is a bad thing, so many test cases/scenarios should be constructed in this area.

Quality Attribute Interoperability
Inter-app The app reviews makes it obvious that Quip could use more testing focus at the points where data is moved in and out of the app. It looks like there are issues with special characters (non-alpha numeric), so tests with input text that contain every ASCII character, and perhaps large samples of other Unicode strings, and multi-language are in order. Test cases should try inserting and exporting these characters via the OS clipboard, from other popular apps. It should be validated that this type of data maintains fidelity via Quip's own sync services, app to app, in real-time. It should also be obvious that Quip should have a large test matrix of moving data in and out of other major text editing apps and services like Dropbox via API. Quip should have a large set of these data interoperability tests as the whole point of Quip is to create and share docs, and not all docs are yet created or shared via Quip. Yet.

Quality Attribute Stability

Unplug All aspects of Quips functionality should be tested offline. Quip testing efforts should create docs and editing them while offline, or with intermittent access. Some testing around data preservation right before the device powers off would go a long way to make sure those last few edits a user makes as their battery warnings are preserved. Tests with multiple clients in offline mode, editing the same text islands would make for some interested data consistency tests. I'm not sure how Quip is written, but this would likely require a mix of network and local storage to accomplish reliably.

Memento The Quip app should be tested under extreme device conditions. Very large documents, and accounts with many documents and folders should be loaded while the device is low or out of storage and with pressures on system memory. Quip should make sure it designs for success which would be a world where users have hundreds or thousands of documents and used on very busy and active user devices on the go.

Squats Like most exercise, this is a set of boring tests, but it is needed. Ideally these tests would be automated, but at least some effort should be made to verify that many app launches, one after the other, are crash and bug free. During some of the app launches, kill the app before the load is completed, you might see partial documents or folder lists, preserved across app launches when the app is shut off during Quip's synchronization at launch time. Be mean to the app and it will share bugs with you.

Cram The Quip app should support very large documents and large sets of these documents. At minimum, testing should discover these limits and understand how the product quality degrades at these boundaries. Load large sets of real-world, or generated documents and document collections. Quip is focused on normal "word" type documents, so pile the teams own documents into the app if you don't have anything secret in there. It might be very interesting to see how it performs loading up many thousands of real-world documents from the web using Google advanced search operators such as "filetype:doc". Concatenating many documents, with rich images and formatting onto themselves and each other to create very large documents, and then testing Quip's performance with load times and formatting changes should prove interesting for the team.

App Quality Monster: Device State and Fragmentation
Flippy Quip is a highly connected app with frequent network pings and connections to 3rd party services such as Google Accounts and Dropbox. A detailed list of all the connection points, and all their possible states should be generated, then use pair-wise testing to flip the states of these OS and external services and verify Quip performs well, with data integrity, under those conditions.

The Dirty The Quip app is all about user and device state. Quip should have a strong suite of tests, automated and manual, that builds on accounts with large amounts of accumulated state. Tests should be run on documents and user accounts that are never deleted, just appended.

App Quality Monster: Users
Tough Love The Quip team obviously has a grand strategy in motion, but it might listen a little closer to feedback on design and feature wishes from end users and respond to those demands more quickly. A good example is the supposed confusion around folder creation and management—perhaps a better UX metaphor than 'folders' would be best suited for this new mobile world. The team would have to listen to feedback and scrap something they obviously invested in heavily. It is often difficult to take tough love comments form early adopters and friends if you spend so much time designing and building it.

App Quality Monster: Competition
App Judo Quip testers should heavily use competitive apps, trying the same document creation, read, update, and delete (CRUD) operations. The team should also focus on signup and data import and export and sync scenarios with other apps. Any perceived gap in functionality, usability, performance, etc, is a bug.

Given that Quip's app is their core business they should also add a bit of automation in thee areas. Also, they would do well to have directed, auto-generated, content Create/Read/Update/Delete (CRUD) test automation may help catch some of apparent data-loss issues.

2E: Development: Apply Quality Attribute and App Tips

Developers always have their hands full, but there are very concrete tips to deal with these app quality issues. The Quip developers should consider these quality driven tips:

Quality Attribute Content
No moldy bread This tip is focused on priority of making sure an app's content is always fresh and updated. The Quip app's quality is largely dependent on complex operations such as simultaneous edits from multiple users and devices. The Quip developers no doubt use algorithmic fanciness similar to what Google Wave employed, but it should be put to the test not just on a white board, but considering real world conditions of end-point unreachability, roll backs, conflicts, and overlapping edits, and serialization of commits that might have a high variance in speed: e.g. user 1 makes and update which starts pushing to the server, while user 2 makes a second update to that same document section, but their update message completes far quicker as they are on a faster net connect. Can these Queues build up? Any algorithmic chance for data inconsistencies? If Quip releases an API (Note: they just did) and these docs are used for more than just human document editing, any sync problems could be amplified. This might be a great case for model-based test development.

Pointcast lives More mundane, but more important, is the load time of the Quip app. If users have to wait for many long seconds to begin editing their documents, they will leave. Creative techniques such as push notifications to proactively push doc updates to all clients, might be useful to minimize the load time the user have to experience, at the cost of power and network of course. Perceived speed is king at the end of the day.

Quality Attribute Interoperability

Inter-app Quip developers should ensure they understand all the entry and exit points for data. Reviews show that extra care needs to be taken via the clipboard APIs. Triple check all documentation around clipboard text formats, rules, exceptions, and make sure your code handles them nicely. Treat 3rd party API integrations such as Dropbox with similar diligence to ensure round trip data fidelity and exception handling.

Quality Attribute Stability
Red Pill Quip's iOS app has some reports of crashing, though not an overwhelming flood of them. Quip's Android app is another story though, with many freezes and hangs in scenarios such as switching apps and launch scenarios. The Quip team should move quickly to ensure they not only have crash SDKs installed, but treat every crash as a top priority issue. No crash is OK, we've learned from the Desktop world that crashes in native apps can lead to security vulnerabilities, data loss, and very unhappy and confused users. If reproduction of issues is difficult, leverage large numbers of crowd testers to hunt down reproductions of crash reports. Today there are awesome tools such as Apptentive.com that will enable the Quip team to respond in real-time to users that might have just experienced a crash or other bug. It is a great chance to have a 2-way conversation to explore just what the user was doing and get some additional information that might aide in a crash reproduction—and apologizing to users. You might even be able to ask them to verify a possible fix before your next release. The key with crashes is never tolerate them--they won't ago away if you ignore them.

A relevant aside: In my old days leading testing for Google Desktop, we had a small number of vocal users reporting that their had drives would just fill up with our index files after a period of many months. Of course, it was almost impossible to debug or reproduce these issues because it was running on someone's personal desktop computer with tons of private data—they couldn't just send us their machine or data to reproduce in our labs. What did we do? Google Desktop indexed almost everything on the machines.. We reached out to those users in the forums, asked them a series of questions like hard drive size, did they use outlook, which OS, which browser, how 'fast' their index file was growing, and tried to see what properties were common among them. This helped us focus on the use of Outlook. Turned out after months of grueling investigations, that a change in the Outlook APIs, not even our code, meant that we no longer generated unique ID's for some objects. So, every time Google Desktop read these items in outlook, it created a new entry instead of updating an old one. A very slow leak that grew as a function of the number of seldom used "Notes" Outlook users added. Heavy users of Outlook notes were impacted. The point of all this is that the hard bugs are just that—hard. Never give up and always have a fanatical focus on quality. Track down every crash like it was a clue to a mystery of the origins of the universe. Never give up on investigations and reproduction attempts—you will eventually figure them out. It is just code and data at the end of the day.

Just do it This tip for the quip team is simple but difficult for most agile teams to execute on. Fix all the crashes you know about. Fix them before any new feature or functional bugs. Fix the crashes.

App Quality Monster: Device State and Fragmentation
Trust Not Quip has many integration points. They have seemingly more integration points with every app release so the risk of API integrations will only get worse for them over time. This is a key candidate for automation as machines can easily validate integration points, and because regressions can happen without a single change in the Quip app when the 3rd party changes their API (see Google Desktop example above). The team will want to validate these integrations continually. The quip team should enumerate all their API integration points, with the system and 3r parties. It may seem strange, but a quick set of API tests for the subset of 3rd party APIs you are using is your best defense. Test for any API contract or behavior changes—only test what you depend on, but do test these 3rd party APIs independent of your app. Importantly, test the failure modes of all your dependencies. Read their documentation about exceptions and error codes, and make sure you app can functionally respond appropriately. Mocks can also be your friend to fake out failures in system or service calls. APIs, especially web service APIs, can and do go down. Even

Google's services go down occasionally, so code defensively. Catch these issues, and handle them in your app, before your users see them.

App Quality Monster: Agile Teams
Backlogs are Dangerous This tip for the Quip team is just to not let bugs build up in the backlog. Perhaps some rules around no feature work unless bugs are fixed would go a long way. Some functional bugs seem to be hanging around a bit longer then they should.

Sunk Costs This is an interesting and emotional tip for most app teams. One example of sunk costs for the Quip team might be its heavy investment the design and implementation of their folder view. Which, as folder views go, is pretty cool and touch friendly. This view though, seems to cause some confusion for users. It is also possibly a legacy metaphor for organizing documents, though even Google Drive couldn't avoid using it either. Perhaps trying a few new design and code variations that de-emphasize the folder UX, or innovatively deprecate the metaphor are worth trying. Too often the desire to focus on the shiny new features and user stories, and the fact that they have pride and an investment in the existing app, keeps teams from revisiting the core of their app with earnest. This is a bold statement from someone not on the Quip team, but it is an example of revisiting sunk costs with a fresh view from time to time, especially when users are saying something is getting in the way of an awesome and intuitive experience.

2F: Product and Design: Apply Quality Attribute and App Tips

Product folks have a lot of influence in both agile sprint planning and deciding on feature completeness. The product folks at Quip might find value in these tips:

Quality Attribute Content
I want it All The Quip team seems to be following the lean startup methodology, at least loosely. Building a new document editor is

no small task. The team did launch a feature rich and well-designed app, but reviews point to many missing integration points and inter-app support, and are sorely missing the ability to bring their existing document libraries into the Quip world. Quip seems to work great at this point if the document is created within Quip and stays in the Quip world, but users want and expect more. Microsoft Word and Apple's Pages support important and export to many different file formats. Perhaps the Quip team was too lean and could have waited for just a bit more feature completeness before launching. Quip was unable to target only early adopters as apps are available to all, so they should make sure they are useful to most everyone before launching, or scare potential users off with some app store description text warning that certain expected features are not yet in the app. Perhaps users would complain less if their expectations were dropped, or avoid the app altogether at this point if they needed these other features—and not share their disappointment in Quip's review stream.

Quality Attribute Interoperability
Inter-app The product folks at Quip should have a very data-driven and prioritized roadmap of integration points for getting data and out of Quip. Even if there is strategic value, or personal interest, in particular an integration point, this roadmap should be heavily influenced by real world user feedback. If only one half of one percent of all users file a review, you may roughly imply that for ever review wishing Quip supported Google Drive integration there might be 200 others silently wishing the same. If user feedback isn't asking for particular integrations, maybe those should be slightly deprioritized. Writing here, I have very little strategic context on Quips plans, but this is a great example for other app teams in how they can leverage app store reviews to influence their product roadmap.

Quality Attribute Stability
Apriority This one is simple. Make sure crashes are prioritized above most every other activity on the app team. Developers should be investigating all known crashes and testers should be looking to find them before your users do. It can be difficult in the agile world to track ongoing crash investigations that might span

many sprints, but make sure you have a user story for 'no crashes'. Prioritize crashes and these embarrassing reviews will eventually go away.

App Quality Monster: Metrics

Just Ask Based on reviews, the Quip team seems to have a great relationship with its users when responding to help requests. As a Quip user, I've yet to see them leverage the power of surveying their power users in-app, or prompting help based on in-app actions such as creating many duplicate folder names, which might be a sign of a functional bug or user frustration. Apptentive.com provides some of this functionality quickly, and might be a great way for Quip to find out just what its users want in the future, and proactively engage them in two-way conversations to resolve any confusion, reproduce issues, and understand their users expectations even better.

App Quality Monster: Competition

Competitive Grid The Quip team surely knows their competition, at least most of it. But the team may not have per-quality attribute visibility into what their competitors are doing better than they are, or looking closely at the likes of what IA Writer and other smaller apps are doing. It is easy to be focused on your own app, but there are tools and methods to track how your app is doing versus the competition. The document editing space is a large one with many upstarts and incumbents, it would pay for Quip to do very deep analysis of competitive apps: user sentiment and features and design.

Clone Wars The IA Writer app has many 5 star reviews referring to their folder design. The IA Writer app used to get 1-star reviews for poor folder support, but its current folder design seems to be generating a lot of positive user feedback. It might be worth the Quip team's time to take a quick peek and see what IA Writer is going right, and clone away.

App Quality Monster: Agile Teams

Bugs over Features This is another simple tip, but difficult to implement. The Quip product folks should be sure they are giving appropriate focus to bug fixing versus features. It looks as if the team has done a good job, as their user sentiment over time has been steadily increasing, but it could likely increase faster with a bit more focus on quality vs. features.

Short Term Thinking This is a meta point, but the pedigree of the Quip team is awesome and full of visionary and technical folks executing on a well-funded and long term mission. But, given that some issues have been in the app store for a while, as new more ambitious features come in, they might benefit from a bit more shorter term thinking—which is part of the idea of being agile. Respond to users quickly. A key example was the fact that they released the iOS app long before the Android app, so they were fine not having platform parity for a while. But, from the outside, the team seems to have slowed iOS releases, and rather than focusing on a perfect iOS quality experience, they instead added new iOS features and built their first version of the Android app with a fair number of quality issues including crashes when it launched. Perhaps the team could have considered less functionality and/or not expanding to other platforms until the iOS app was a 4- or 5-star app.

3A: Execution: Measuring Build vs. Build Quality

Most importantly, the Quip team should look to see that when this extra testing, crash fixing and interoperability feature design is released into the app stores, that their star ratings actually improve, and that there are fewer complaints and more praise in the app store from their users. The plot of user sentiment based quality should move up and to the right. The team should never tolerate losing ground in stars.

The next step is to rinse and repeat until you have 4.9 stars—you can never be perfect in they eyes of all people. GOTO 1A.

For those app teams still working on their first version, or don't have any app reviews yet, much of this analysis is still valuable, perhaps more valuable. Look at the data for your planned app's category to see what areas to really nail before your release date. Analyze your competitors before you even launch—see what their users love and complain about, so you can learn and launch with a better app and star rating right out of the gate.

As promised, here is a quick bit of analysis that we couldn't do with Quip because it had too few reviews. For apps with many reviews coming in each day or week, it can be difficult to keep track of them all. You can use a spreadsheet, or you can use clustering built into analytis.applause.com. Lets look at some of the review clusters for a favorite app of mine that just launched a with a major UX re-design: Starbucks.

Review Cluster, 1-Star, Count 12, 3/14-4/14, Starbucks, iOS: "HATE HATE HATE the new app...wish there was a way to give negative stars.Cannot even do basis things like search for the nearest store with..."

Review Cluster, 1-Star, Count 5, 4/14-4/14, Starbucks, iOS: "Whats the point of having the app if there's no menu?"

Review Cluster, 1-Star, Count 5, 3/14-4/14, Starbucks, iOS: "I've now reentered my email address and cant sign in"

Review Cluster, 1.-Star, Count 4, 4/14-4/14, Starbucks, iOS: "I finally got the update today after being prompted by the old version everytime i tried to use it. And guess what, the app did not even start once for me. Just crashes everytime so I cant even use it..."

Review Cluster, 1-Star, Count 8, 3/14-4/14, Starbucks, iOS: "I discovered my saved stars are gone…"

Here you can see the most frequent types of review feedback that the Starbucks app team is getting from their users. You can see how many reviews are in each cluster, when that cluster of reviews started, and possibly ended. Lets analyze a couple of these review clusters and think about what the Starbucks app team should be focusing on right now:

- **Drink Menu and Nutrition information is gone**: In the old app there was a goofy UX that let you make a drink. You could pick a latte; add a splash of vanilla, and extra shot. You could save this drink as a favorite and check out the calorie count. It wasn't much more useful than that—you couldn't scan it and the barista automatically knew what you wanted, but some folks liked it. The update didn't have this functionality—and didn't message this nicely to users. With the new app design, users hunted around for their drinks UI, couldn't find it, and started complaining. The team might at least consider a place holder in the app saying 'sorry its gone', or 'be patient, a more awesome one is coming later', or just add it back in.
- **Sign in Issues**: The update didn't preserve users' sign in credentials. So, existing users were suddenly forced to sign in again, and when an app forces this, many folks will have forgotten their password. There could also be a functional regression bug with sign in, but it is more likely just folks forgetting their password, and the app having a poor, or missing, password recovery path.
- **Saved Stars are Gone**: Users are saying they lost their stars. Coffee nuts get stars for every dink they purchase and after collecting a few of them, they are redeemable for, you guessed it, more free coffee. Real or not, users are thinking the update just cost them money and they aren't happy about it.

In general, it doesn't look like the team did much beta feedback, or focus on the sign in flows that have plagued the app for a long time, or considering the migration of users to the new app UI. It is easier for app teams to start clean with a new build, but your users have state and expectations—disappoint them at your peril.

Lets also look at another important aspect of reviews that we couldn't see with Quip, because they have so few reviews coming in—the app sentiment, positive versus negative, over time. You often see major inflection points in this graph when new builds are released into the app store. Can you guess when the new fancy UX redesign launched? Watch for these inflection points in your own app and respond quickly!

Summary

We've done a lot without even talking to the Quip team, or Starbucks team. The app's code, their feature and triage lists or test cases. This is a demonstration of the power that modern app teams have at their disposal by combining best practices with data-driven quality assessments. Use this power for good.

Section VI: Future of App Quality

"Winter is coming."
— George R.R. Martin, A Game of Thrones

Even the best app teams today still treat app quality with an ad-hoc collection of agile process, tools, SDKs, dashboards, humans and machines. The world of desktop and web apps within companies slowly moved toward vertical integrations of these systems to bring much of this build and project quality tracking together into a pluggable, if not unified system. In mobile, this integration is happening more quickly, and the resulting systems will be far more efficient and intelligent given the consolidation in platforms, and the data available in the app stores.

The intelligent platform for App Quality Management, perhaps called an AQM (Application Quality Monitoring) system, will know more about the quality issues and strengths about your app than you do. This is largely due the ability to centrally collect production feedback via SDKs and app store reviews, along with the rapid consolidation in tools for measuring performance, engagement, and monetization. This instrumentation will be deployed across the full lifecycle of design, build, testing (automated and human), with beta programs, and production monitoring. There are three major opportunities to improve quality and efficiency with mobile apps:

1. **Deep Quantification of Quality** Engagement, monetization, performance, even subjective user sentiment—all of these are now deeply quantified by commodity or free services.
2. **Efficient Distribution and Agile** Consolidation in app development toolsets, and the commoditization and automation of app distribution will give many app teams the ability to release quickly, based on near-real-time quality feedback. This rapid release cycle also adds additional data points with which to track quality at an even more detailed level, with higher confidence, and the ability

to track quality metrics back to specific and isolated changes in the app.

3. **Analytics** Data and analytics will span the applications lifecycle, as well as across the app ecosystem. This richness of data across the application lifecycle allows for predictive analytics to understand how your app will fare when pushed to production. The app store level analytics enables app teams to benchmark their app's quality to their category, and even perform direct competitive analysis against other apps.

The days of big empty bug and work item databases like JIRA, HP Quality Center, IBMs Rational or Microsoft's TFS are coming to an end unless they adapt to this new world. Future systems for app development will be smart, predictive and proactively advise app teams on where to focus. An intelligent assistant or consultant will soon emerge from within app toolsets.

App World Acceleration

The adoption of mobile devices has outpaced the rise of PCs and even the browsers of the past. This rapid change will only accelerate--until the singularity that is. Here are the issues this will bring to app teams:

- **Increasingly Rapid builds** Just a few years ago, monthly releases were deemed aggressive. Today weekly and even daily builds and deploys are commonplace with Continuous Integration systems. This acceleration will again minimize the value from classical manual testing efforts, as there just isn't enough time to evaluate a build manually before the next build is ready for testing. That next build adds entropy/churn into the investigation of any failures found during manual testing. Humans need to be aided by smarter test automation, build inspection, code analysis and analytics to point them to the interesting places in the app more quickly. We welcome our automated and analytical robot overlords.

- **Cross-Platform** The novelty of mobile apps has worn off. Mobile apps are now just another client, an extension of the larger app or service. Users will want to move seamlessly between devices and environments, and expect their apps and services to adapt to them in real-time. This will put further pressure on app teams to design for multi-platform, greatly increase development costs, further complicate testing matrices, and drive the need to centralize all application lifecycle management systems into one.

- **Internet of Things and the rise of Complexity** As the size of devices drop to zero, and the number of these devices explode, the need for centralized and coordinating software will appear. Simple systems like IFTTT https://ifttt.com/ may rise to fill this need, but even then, every app, or node, needs to be programmable, and communicate on this new smart data app layer. This increases both the complexity of each node to know how to behave and interact with other nodes and services, peer-to-peer, as well as the compatibility and versioning black hole that we saw in the desktop COM world. This time it will be orders of magnitude more difficult. The quality danger will also increase, as these devices will communicate with your lights—turning lights off while walking down stairs isn't a great idea. Auto starting your car in the winter, when it is in the garage isn't a great idea either. We may see network-level complexity appearing in our decentralized apps in the coming years. Good old N^2.

- **Internet of Things and Relevance** As apps disappear into our walls, wallets, cars, glasses, shoes and watches, the number of signals coming into our lives will grow many-fold. Most people thought their inboxes were exploding when the world came online. Just wait until every object and virtual service treats us as addressable nodes on the network, fighting for our attention. There will be pressure on each service or app to avoid spamming or risk being muted. As these apps will travel everywhere we go, and be everywhere we go, and will interact with everything around us, even more intelligence will be expected of our apps—to make our interaction with them relevant. The explosion in data can also be used to improve the relevance of these interrupts. The next generation of App quality will become less about features, capabilities, and UX, and more about delivering relevant information at the right time to the right person, in the right place. App quality will soon become similar to the quality problem of Google Search-where everything about you is the query, your entire world of data is the index, and it is the app job to rank all this information and only deliver it to you at the perfect moment. "Google Now" is a peek into that future.

Application Quality Management (AQM) Workflows

Increasingly, app teams demand real-time data across their infrastructure. More focus will be on understanding not just the absolute level of quality of a build, but focusing rather on whether the new build is better than the last one—hyper agile teams want know if they should stop the auto-deploy of their app to users. Let's walk through an idealized, next-gen agile, AQM system. Lets review the parts, and the flow.

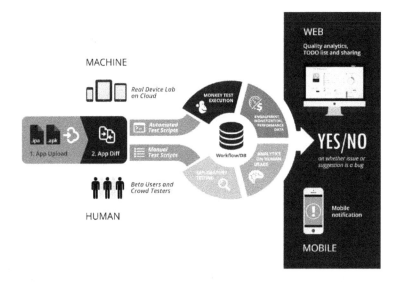

APP Upload

This is where it all begins--with the app binary. During App Upload, the binary is pushed from the build system into the Mobile Agile flow. This binary is automatically instrumented with code to measure and control the app along its journey through the system. Instrumentation such as engagement analytics, device information, and app management is added magically to the binary—no need to add code or libraries to your build process.

App Diff

If the app team knew what changed between the current and the last build, everything else is easy. If the developer could know within minutes how her code change impacted the app's UX or behavior, she could verify that her changes worked. If the tester knows what changed, they would have a list of bugs, validations, or clues as to where the regressions likely live. The more frequently this flow is executed the easier it is to isolate what changes caused regressions or improvements. If this flow is kicked for every single check-in, the app team also immediately knows the source of the change—the last check-in. This is a major step in efficiency and quality for developers and testers alike. The AQM provides a service that automatically compares the newest build to the last build version. AQM's will leverage the dramatic drop in compute and storage costs to minimize the amount of human labor, which is more expensive than ever. The App Diff service mechanically identifies differences between the builds in two fundamental ways:

1. **Inspection**: The app diff service peeks inside the android APK file, or the iOS IPA file, and finds the XML or plist info that describes the UX of the app. If something was removed, app diff knows it. If something new appears, app diff knows it. If something changed position or size, app diff knows. With the definition of the UX elements, app diff can even draw a picture of what the change looks like. Not every app uses the tools to define their app's UX, but most do. The standardization of app tooling and binary formats makes this plausible in the modern app world.

2. **Behavioral**: the app diff service also wakes up and starts driving the app like a crazy monkey. Literally a UX monkey that sends semi-intelligent gestures and taps to buttons on the screen to explore the app. For every build, the monkey keeps track of what view was loaded, message sent, or action happened when it clicked on the same button in an older build. If something is behaviorally different with the new build, app diff takes a picture, and reports the behavioral difference. Yes, this is more difficult than it sounds, but that's the fun of it, and the reward in quality and efficiency will be dramatic.

All these little 'diffs' are then immediately presented to both the developer and the tester for evaluation. Is this a feature, or a bug? This is a pretty simple question for a human, but difficult for a machine. The old adage is that a bug fix is far less expensive if it is caught earlier. App diff can catch regressions and feature validations in near real-time.

Humans: Dogfood, Crowd, Beta, and Production Users

Apps should be like people: rude to their family, sort of nice to their neighbors, and super polite to strangers. Give your early app builds to yourself and your team to find the earliest bugs. If things look OK, pass that build on to your early adopters, testers, and crowd testers to look for issues. Only after everyone else has seen the app, share it with the public.

Your app team is like your family. Just as your family knows a lot about you, and can tolerate many of your day to say idiosyncrasies, and your app team dogfooding will give you very candid feedback and tolerate bad builds. Your friends are much like your testers and beta users. Your, testers, early adopters and the crowd, give less detailed feedback, but it is often constructive. Like strangers, your public users will often complain to themselves quietly and simply move on—deleting your app without a whisper. Those strangers that do complain will complain very publicly with graffiti on your app's review stream.

The feedback from humans is often much slower than that from machines, but it has far more context and depth than stack traces and false positive failures from automation test scripts. Humans can also hunt down issues that test scripts cannot find or understand. Today's app quality world is even more dependent on subjective and qualitative issues—you need the human brain. Human feedback is critical, as we have not yet developed sentient machines, because your app's users, at the end of the day, are humans. You need to know the human angle.

Humans are also needy—they often need to be told what to focus on. In an agile environment, that shiny new build will often look just like the last build. Humans need more context on what is new in this build or they will inefficiently wander aimlessly—or get bored. The AQM system will feed app diff data, app store review complaints (and praises), best practices and suggestions, to the app team and its testers. The AQM will even push the build and this testing context directly to their device, perhaps even loading the app and taking them to the app view with the new changes automagically. Humans are slow, but put them in the right place with the right context within your app and they are the most valuable quality signal available.

The modern AQM will support automatic distribution of your app through various stages of users, with increasing quality and ever more context. The AQM will monitor their feedback and engagement and decide whether that app build should progress further, or halt it in its tracks and interrupt the app team to take care of an issue.

Unlike ALM's of the past, AQM systems will provide crowd testers available as a service. For modern apps, the ability to execute tests with varying device contexts, different demographics and located in the real world, vs. the lab, is vital, not just an interesting option. Many app teams today and in the future are often too small, or too focused on their feature work to hire, mentor and support a dedicated test team.

Manual Test Scripts

Manual test scripts have existed forever, and their half-life has been pegged at 10 years each of the last three decades. Manual test scripts just aren't going away. They will be with us for a long time. Test cases haven't evolved much, they can and should be smarter and delivered more effectively.

Test Case Delivery Today, test scripts are often stored in a giant database, or spreadsheet, and read from a web page or, gasp, sometimes from a desktop client. In an app world, this is awkward. Apps are supposed to be convenient, mobile, and contextual. Apps are fully functional clients but they aren't treated with as much respect. Build a separate app client to show the test cases? No...because switching apps is painful and slow. Notifications allow for dissemination of test steps in real time, to the device a tester is holding. Notifications can also present themselves on top of the application under test. Test cases should be delivered directly to the device and the app via push notification and clicking that notification should launch the app under test automatically. Why not? The app should also be opened to as close to the state where the human brain needs to be involved. The app should be launched, signed in with the testing account, and auto navigate to the search box with the text for the text case pre-populated—asking the tester to hit 'go', and user their intuition and subjectivity to validate the correctness of the results. The days of test cases living outside of the app are coming to a glorious end.

Bug Filing: Manual test delivery is a two-way street. How do we get the results of the test case back to the test case database? Click on a pass button or link on desktop web page? Again, the AQM will leverage the new world of app infrastructure and all its convenience. The notification itself can host the UX for a quick PASS/FAIL. Even fancier, an SDK living inside the app can enable test logging UX inside the app itself. If the result is PASS, great, send the tester the next test case via notification. If it is a FAIL, the flow should screenshot the app, allow the user to draw notes on the screenshot, and automatically attach all application breadcrumbs, device state, and push this back up to the server.

Why the world still types in data that can be gathered automagically just goes to show that testing technology stopped evolving about 10 years ago.

Distribution: Modern app teams, even small ones, can quickly accumulate hundreds of test cases that they'd like executed before each new release. How do you distribute these? App teams have N testers and M test cases. During test passes, they simply assign M/N tests to each tester. This means the test cycle will take as long as the slowest tester. In an agile world, this just isn't good enough for fast moving agile teams. If test cases are independent of each other, they should be distributed on a first-come first-serve basis off a global test case queue.

Auto Test Cases and Test Selection We know so much more about testing and quality than we did 10 years ago, but it is passed around as folklore on blogs and anecdotally in books like this one. The AQM will draw on a database of best practices, including test cases and testing tours and tips and tricks like the ones listed above in this book. Each test case and tour (for directed exploratory testing) will be associated with specific quality attributes or key words, so the system can look at the collection of all data known about the app (test cases, bugs, app store reviews, work items, code descriptions, app category, competitive apps) and generate a prioritized list of suggested test cases that should be executed. The AQM has a tester-in-a-box, and it just might be as effective as ones that you interview, pay, and manage on-site. In this way, the AQM can generate a basic test strategy, built on best practices, specific to your app, in seconds.

Definition: Exploratory testing is an approach to software testing that is concisely described as simultaneous learning, test design and test execution. Cem Kaner, who coined the term in 1983, now defines exploratory testing as "a style of software testing that emphasizes the personal freedom and responsibility of the individual tester to continually optimize the quality of his/her work by treating test-related learning, test design, test execution, and test result interpretation as mutually supportive activities that run in parallel throughout the project." --Wikipedia

Test Execution Context Context is everything. Most tests are executed blindly, and quickly, without knowing the larger picture of app quality. What has changed in this build (scrum notes, code check-in explanations, app store reviews with text relating to the test case description, this test's PASS/FAIL history, how many other testers have been at this same place within the app, how many testers have found bugs executing this test on other platforms or devices, etc.) The more context the better the testing and bug reporting will be. The AQM's job is to share as much relevant context as possible to the tester during test execution at just the right time and place.

Analytics on Human Usage

The AQM will perform deep analytics on the length of time spent on each test case and proactively analyze bug-filing for further scheduling and learning. Summaries of the device matrix and app state coverage are almost as important as the test results. Knowing who tested your app, where they were, what devices they used, what state their devices where in, and what they did within the app individually and in aggregate is critical to understanding the confidence in your app's success when it gets to production.

Machines in the Cloud

Regression test automation on devices is becoming more important every day for modern apps. App teams can't keep up with the device matrix, nor have the time to manage a lab of devices, have the time to write reams of test cases, nor have the patience to wait for test results from humans. Machines are great at large scale breadth testing, regression validation, and most importantly speed. Machines are fast, which means the time between a developer checking in code, and a CI system producing a build, to getting preliminary results on whether she can leave the building, or needs to revert her code change can be minutes in the app world. This should all sound very familiar to Web and Desktop app developers, but this level of sophistication and tooling is just now reaching the mobile app world. Most notably different is the fragmentation issue—you need to use cloud machines, managed by 3rd parties, to efficiently keep up with the changing landscape of devices. Machines in the cloud are leveling the playing field for app teams as every team, large and small, struggles with the device matrix.

Automated Monkey Tests

Some monkeys are less intelligent than others. Much like the Google Chrome leverages large scale crash detection systems that look for simple crashes across millions of URLs, the modern AQM will automatically run the app through its basic paces of install, launch, and random gestures across a large set of devices. This provides near real-time feedback on the quality of the build, catches major regressions before more expensive machines or humans are involved, and importantly requires about zero setup or configuration from the app team. The speed of results will enable agile teams to continue coding and building as fast as they like.

Note: The monkeys might be stuck at the gate. For apps, like Netflix, that require sign in, the test build should either auto-sign in with a testing account, or a tiny automated script that performs sign in should be created, to let the monkey's in to attack the app's primary functionality.

Automated Regression Scripts

The AQM will support functional API, and UX-based test regression. Like classic ALM systems, the AQM, will support the programmatic distribution, prioritization, and analysis of regression automation. Unlike legacy ALMs, AQMs will natively support the direct execution of these tests on cloud machines under its control—as a service. Also unlike previous ALMs where product teams would purchase hardware, and pick test frameworks and manage them manually, the AQM service will provide this execution capacity as a commodity service. App teams want to be more focused on their app and their features, and less on the commodity aspects of execution—especially as non-software companies and many more vendors are jumping into the app development fray. Everyone has to have an app, but not everyone should have to maintain a test lab full of devices and test engineers.

Production Analytics

An app's quality isn't confined to its functional correctness. The quality of an app is ultimately measured in how engaged the users are, what they purchase via the app, and how it contributes to internal company KPIs. KPI's are data such as increased awareness of corporate information, reduced support costs, reduced churn and abandonment across their services, and increased deal throughput by the companies the sales force.

These non-traditional quality metrics can now be tied directly to product design, reliability, and performance issues as they too are quantified. The key value of the AQM is to look for causal relations in the data. Did that increase in server latency cause a corresponding drop in revenue, or app store ratings? Did that new UX change drive move users to discover and use in-app purchases? Did the new streaming video functionality in the app lead to more, or larger sales deals this quarter? Analytics that relate these various quality metrics is the primary job of the AQM. The days of "I think it is a better app, and that might somehow add value to the business" are ending soon.

Workflow / DB

The brain of the AQM is a basic workflow engine and analytics dB where all the relatable data, and best practices are stored. The AQM orchestrates the mechanics of getting a build, and then conditionally routing that build, with various context, to all components in the ALM. Remember all those emails about "The BVT results are in, send it out to the test team', or "Is this build better than the last one?" The AQM will make these mails a relic of the past.

Tip Map

The AQM will proactively generate tips, and suggestions to the app team. ALMs of the past simply recorded your data and charted it back for you on demand.

The AQM will proactively triage and rank the app teams' bug and work items lists. Today's ALMs simply rely on the app team's guess at relative severity and priority, often without global quality context. The AQM will have the global quality context and will suggest prioritization with justifications out of the box. The AQM will suggest tests or code or design suggestions based on best practices and data gleaned from hundreds of other apps and the relations it sees between your bug and work items with app store reviews and relations with your teams KPIs.

The AQM will also proactively ensure the app team gets the right best practices at the right time. If the app is suffering from a large number of crashes, for instance, the AQM will:

- Increase priority to bug reports of crashes
- Show how crashes are impacting retention KPIs, revenue, and app store star ratings.
- Suggest a set of test cases that target common crash scenarios
- Suggest tips to developers on adding crash detection SDKs, and analyzing crash reports, and sharing platform-specific coding best practices and robust libraries.
- Notify you when the crash metrics, and business KPIs actually get better, and to focus on the next big thing.

Clients

The AQM client is as important as the infrastructure. The AQM client is where the system presents the product team with a combined view of bugs, tips, and quality metrics. The client performs two major functions:

1. **Present the data in a compelling context**. If there is a simple bug with signing into the app, it will show that bug, along with data that suggests this issue is important to fix as it impacts engagement metrics and $N dollars of revenue.
2. **Present the opportunity for basic learning**. App teams are all very different. Some for the better and some for the worse. Some app teams just won't ever care about the elegance of their app's UX. These folks will initially see strong suggestions that their app needs a makeover, but business goals, or other priorities might mean this just won't happen. Next to every piece of data presented by the AQM, the user has the opportunity to thumbs up or thumbs down the class of suggestions and data. Over time, the AQM will suppress prioritization of bugs, tips, and analytics related to elegance. The AQM will adapt to different app teams. Netflix learns your preference for romantic tearjerker movies; why not also auto-tune our very expensive software design and engineering projects?

Visualization

Everyone likes to think they have lots of data and charts and graphs available to make decisions. The reality is that these charts are rarely understood, or monitored, systematically by the actual people that can make the changes needed for great app quality. They let the crash reports or the review alerts pile up, and maybe they put them into the backlog. Quality data such as bugs and crash reports and test cases can be boring. Charts and graphs can be intimidating and take a fair amount of mental muscle to device actionable meaning. The next generation AQM needs to convey the message in as clear and succinct and engaging a way as possible. What makes chart and graphs and statistics compelling to even the laziest reader at a Starbucks café--A USA Today style infographic. The AQM of the future will have far more impact than systems of old as its data will be engaging, personalized, and pretty enough to print and put on the cubicle wall. Here is an early example of a personalized infographic, automatically generated for every app in the app store based on the data and tips and tricks contained in this book.

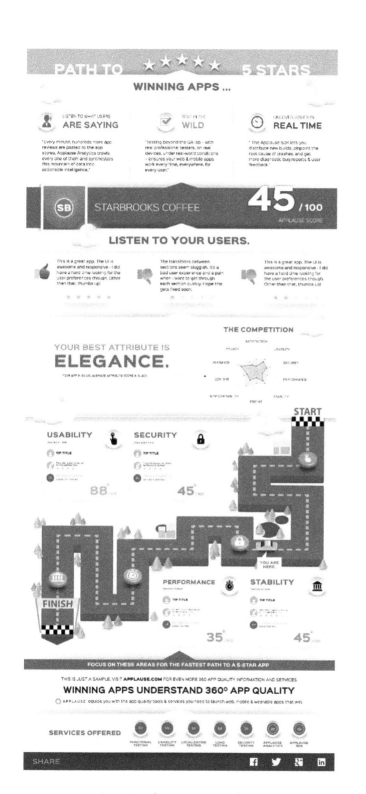

App Quality: Secrets for Agile App Teams 303

The AQM of the near future will accelerate app quality and enable app teams to focus more of their time on their app design, features and users.

If you have enjoyed this book, please leave a review in the Amazon Kindle or iBook store. If you found issues with it, or have suggestions, or disagreements, please email me instead of posting a review ☺

Section VII: Homies (credits)

Applause Analytics Team

The analytics.applause.com team:

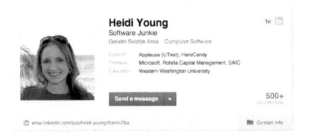

Heidi Young's official title is Director of Data, but she's really a product manager, developer, and analytics guru all rolled into one. Her ability to iterate on complex data, design and customers all in the same afternoon has assured swift progress and adoption of the app store review analytics. Heidi is continually driving the team's goal of creating a machine that passes the 'Tester Turing Test'— building a system that knows more about an app's quality than the test manager of the app. She probably knows more about your app than you do :)

Jason Stredwick is the master of all trades and the jack of none. Jason has owned the core analytics compute and scaling issues for applause.com. He won't admit it, but he's also done some UX work in his time. Jason is the unsung hero of everything applause.com engineering.

Jeff Carollo does the hard work of building out the 'first' of most everything. Jeff wrote the first app store crawler (destroying Google App Engine's map reduce functionality in the process), the first review scorer, the first applause Android app, and recently the first example of auto-injecting mobile SDKs into android APK files. If there is a technical challenge, Jeff is solving it. The more difficult the challenge, the sooner Jeff seems to get a demo up and running.

Sebastian Schiavone-Ruthensteiner is the product manager that can take any raw data and envision a product and service. Sebastian does a lot of the meta-thinking around product and go-to market, but also digs deep and gets his hands dirty. As we were developing applause.com's core scoring algorithm, Sebastian personally read and categorized many thousands of reviews and painstakingly looked for patterns in the data. Really, applause.com's scoring is just another instantiation of his brain. Sebastian had the most critical realization of all—it is not just about bugs, but realizing that users are saying positive and awesome things about apps too. Those positive reviews are as just as value as the negative.

Joe Mikhail is the quiet genius who runs a data center out of his condo in downtown San Francisco. Joe writes the code that manages over 1000 web crawlers on amazons EC2, which crawl the Google Play and Apple App Stores every day. Joe spends much of his time making sure his machines look like docile and polite machines to avoid being banned as bots, and responding to all the schema and operational changes by the DevOps at Google and Apple. It is a quiet, ongoing technical battle thanks for Joe. Most crawl and index teams are teams. At applause.com, it is just Joe.

Matthew Johnson defines the applause analytics product and UX---and builds it! Matthew has transformed the product form a bunch of graphs and charts into a beautiful and intuitive analytics product that has customer feedback teams at some of the largest app companies saying things like "this product is my job description" :) The product today needs very little introduction or explanation thanks for Matthews's tireless work to make it slick and obvious, actionable, and high quality.

Rhan Kim is the humble and quiet innovator that worked to make the App Store analytics data, and much of this book material, programmatically accessible via APIs. Her APIs now power some of the largest app quality efforts in the world. She also drove the definition and execution of the infographic project, which makes much of this data accessible, actionable, and visually engaging. Rhan is the master of turning data-nerd charts and graphs into something that real app teams, and CTO's, and CIO's will actually look at and motivate them to take action. Without Rhan, much of this data and knowledge would be trapped in these pages—she figured out how to get it out to the world. It is rare that someone can understand UX, the customer, the data, and even hand code APIs herself.

uTest Team

uTest is a crowd-testing company that tests hundreds of apps, via thousands of testers (100k+ registered), for many of the top app companies today.

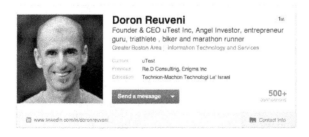

Doron Reuveni, the CEO of uTest, approached me after a talk I gave at GTAC (Google Test Automation Conference) and asked what I was working on in the near future. I surprised him by saying I was likely going to leave Google soon to work on a startup idea I had. Doron suggested I consider working with uTest. We quickly worked out a deal were we created a labs team in Seattle (uTest is based in Boston), free from oversight to focus and experiment in the general area of 'quantifying quality'. A few months later, I left Google with four other Googlers. We knew mobile apps were exploding in numbers and impact on our daily lives. We also quickly learned that very few best practices or knowledge existed around mobile apps. Throughout our experimentation, Duron treated our office like a true "labs", free from monetization pressure, and the freedom to experiment and let failed experiments die quietly. Doron is one of the few true supporters of innovation I've met in a career that spans many startups, Microsoft and Google.

Roy Solomon founded uTest on the idea of having a spreadsheet in the cloud, where customers can post their testing needs and testers around the world could post bugs and test case results. Somewhere in between he'd collect a few pennies from the transaction. During my stay at uTest, I've seen Roy successfully navigate uTest through the mobile revolution, going from 20% of revenue from mobile app testing, to now close to 70%, keeping uTest's platform at the tip of the mobile spear the entire journey. Including the aggressive acquisition and integration of the Apphance SDK (now Applause SDK). Roy was patient as the Seattle team meandered through different product variations and customer feedback iterations. As the data and product matured, Roy drove the Seattle team to explore practical channels for distribution via channels like IBM, awareness, and ultimately direct integration into the core uTest platform. Roy's support was critical to incubate our work, as well as bring it to market so it could make an impact on the hundreds of customers and apps that uTest processes every month.

Rich Weiss is a marketing genius and turns complex products like Applause Analytics and into sweet and simple messages. Rich is also an honorary Product Manager and designer as his musings and whiteboard drawings keep turning into features. If you catch Rich wearing a bow tie, please don't stare.

Me, Jason Arbon

Crowd Testers

These top mobile crowd testers shared what they have learned from testing hundreds of apps and filing literally thousands of bugs.

Alexander Waldman, Germany

Sammy Iqbal, Netherlands

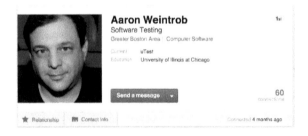

Aaron Weintrob, USA

Georgios Boletis, Greece

Image Attributions

All flat, black and white icons, are pulled directly from
http://www.flaticon.com. Or are custom mashups of icons I made
from them. Specific artists are

- *"Icon made by Freepik from Flaticon.com"*
- *"Icon made by Icomoon from Flaticon.com"*
- *"Icon made by Zurb from Flaticon.com"*
- *"Icon made by Adam Whitcroft from Flaticon.com"*
- *"Icon made by vectorgraphit from Flaticon.com"*
- *"Icon made by Daniel Bruce from Flaticon.com"*
- *"Icon made by Appzgear from Flaticon.com"*
- *"Icon made by Mobiletuxedo from Flaticon.com"*
- *"Icon made by Dave Gandy from Flaticon.com"*
- *"Icon made by Elegant Themes from Flaticon.com"*
- *"Icon made by SimpleIcon from Flaticon.com"*
- *"Icon made by Situ Herrera from Flaticon.com"*
- *"Icon made by Freepik from Flaticon.com"*
- *"Icon made by OCHA from Flaticon.com"*
- *"Icon made by Yannick from Flaticon.com"*
- *"Icon made by Scott de Jonge from Flaticon.com"*

Appendix A: Attribute Distribution Per Category

Quality Attribute Analysis: books

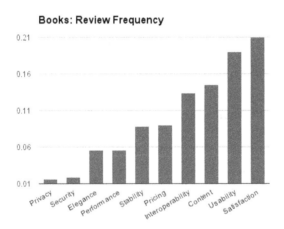

Quality Attribute Analysis: Catalogs

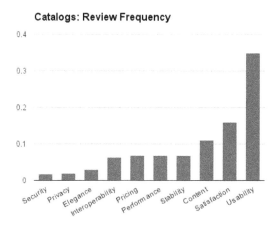

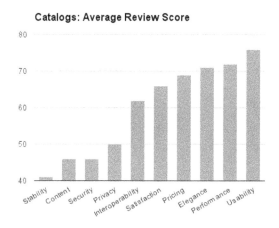

Quality Attribute Analysis: Education

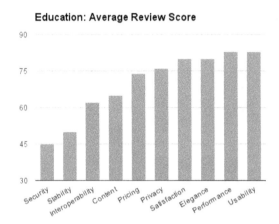

Education: Average Review Score

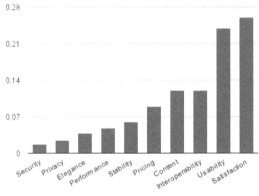

Education: Review Frequency

Quality Attribute: Entertainment

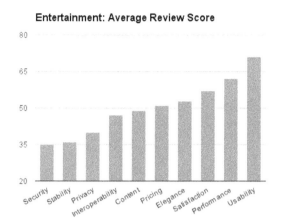

Entertainment: Average Review Score

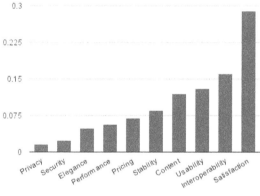

Entertainment: Review Freqency

Quality Attribute Analysis: Finance

Finance: Average Review Score

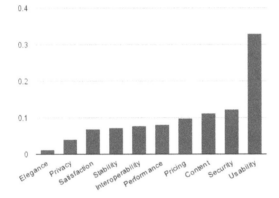

Finance: Review Frequency

Quality Attribute Analysis: Food and Drink

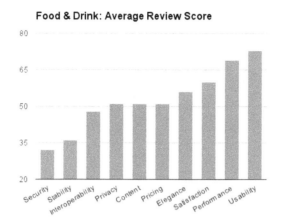

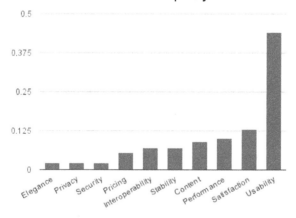

Quality Attribute Analysis: Games

Games: Average Review Score

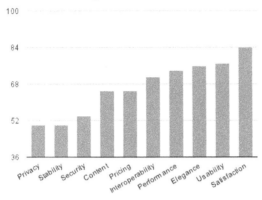

Games: Review Frequency

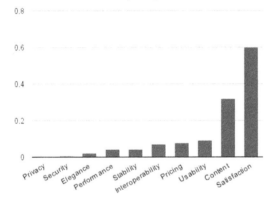

Quality Attribute Analysis: Health and Fitness

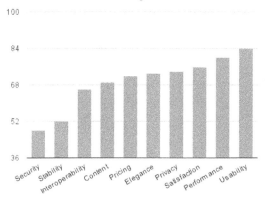

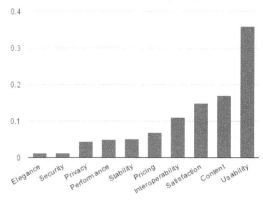

Quality Attribute Analysis: Lifestyle

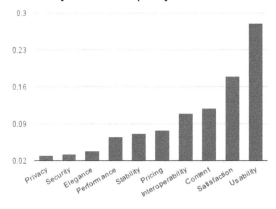

Quality Attribute Analysis: Medical

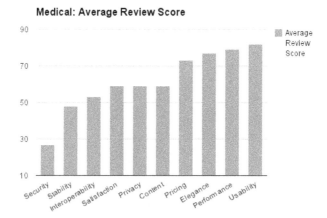

Medical: Average Review Score

Medical: Review Frequency

Quality Attribute Analysis: music

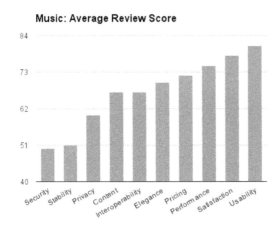

Music: Average Review Score

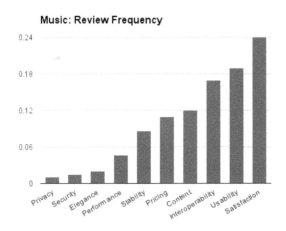

Music: Review Frequency

Quality Attribute Analysis: Navigation

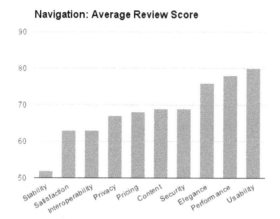

Navigation: Average Review Score

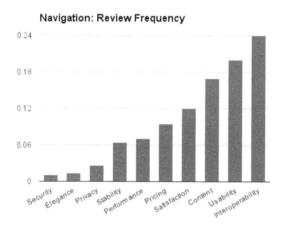

Navigation: Review Frequency

Quality Attribute Analysis: News

News: Average Review Score

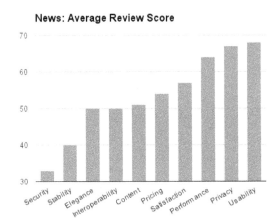

News: Review Frequency

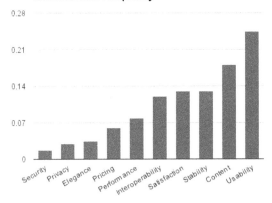

Quality Attribute Analysis: Photo & video

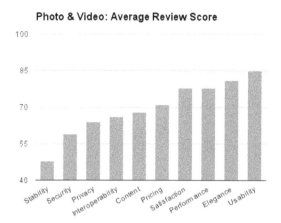

Photo & Video: Average Review Score

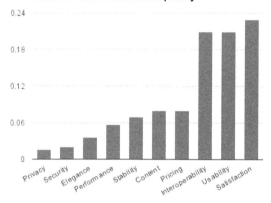

Photo & Video: Review Frequency

Quality Attribute Analysis: Productivity

Productivity: Average Review Score

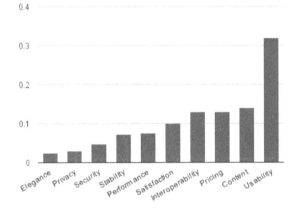

Productivity: Review Frequency

Quality Attribute Analysis: Reference

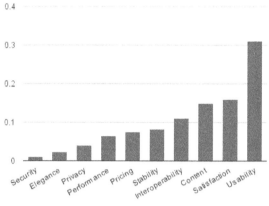

Reference: Review Frequency

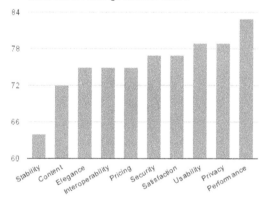

Reference: Average Review Score

Quality Attribute Analysis: Social Networking

Social Networking: Average Review Score

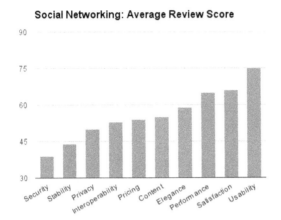

Social Networking: Review Frequency

Quality Attribute Analysis: Sports

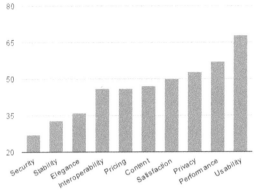

Sports: Average Review Score

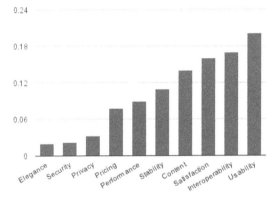

Sports: Review Frequency

Quality Attribute Analysis: Travel

Travel: Average Review Score

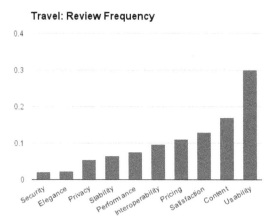

Travel: Review Frequency

Quality Attribute Analysis: Utilities

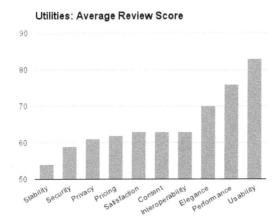

Utilities: Average Review Score

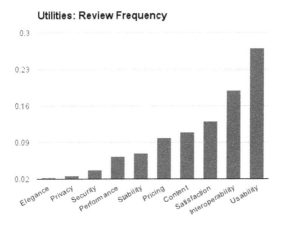

Utilities: Review Frequency

Quality Attribute Analysis: Weather

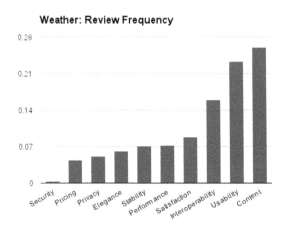

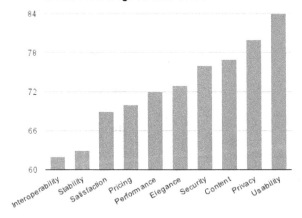

If you made it this far, you obviously care about app quality. If you have additional ideas on how to improve the world of app quality, ping me @jarbon. Cheers.

Index

B

C

D

E

F

G

H

I

J

N

O

P

Q

R

resolution · 26, 117
Respect Authority · 217
Restoration · 176
Retentive · 167, 277
Reverse Engineer · 57
Reviews · 4, 7, 16, 74, 75, 76, 78, 83, 87, 103, 110, 131, 159, 166, 174, 183, 188, 191, 207, 213, 229, 271, 281
ReWork · 71
Rex Hartson · 64, 146
Rich Weiss · 230, 313
Robi Ganguly · 89
Robotium · 255
Roy Solomon · 312

S

Sad Pandas · 208
Salesforce · 52
Sammy Iqbal, Netherlands · 314
Satisfaction · 5, 90, 100, 206, 210, 234, 262, 272
SauceLabs · 254
Scale Pixels · 217
Schrodinger's Quality · 47
Screen · 28, 131, 215
SDK · 37, 47, 48, 49, 50, 116, 121, 122, 149, 151, 155, 156, 186, 215, 297, 312
sdk.applause · 31, 37, 50
SDKs · 6, 37, 41, 47, 48, 49, 50, 57, 113, 116, 121, 122, 151, 193, 281, 290, 303, 309
Sebastian Schiavone-Ruthensteiner · 309
Secret · 184
Security · 4, 5, 16, 50, 65, 100, 190, 195, 200, 203, 233, 234, 235
Selenium · 251, 255
server · 20, 34, 45, 50, 98, 105, 108, 109, 114, 118, 126, 136, 150, 152, 165, 168, 171, 185, 200, 201, 203, 240, 263, 273, 280, 298, 301
Settings · 28
Share It · 31
Short Term Thinking · 73, 286
Sign in Caution · 194
Signals · 4, 100, 101, 103, 107, 130, 147, 158, 165, 173, 182, 190, 206, 212, 234
Signing Paperwork · 21
Siri · 210
Snapchat · 110, 185, 191, 192
Soasta · 149
SOC2 · 50
Social · 28, 40, 237, 332
Sounds · 28
Spam · 86
Spotify · 214

T

X

Y

Z

App Quality: Secrets for Agile App Teams